Battling Choices

Yotam Gadot

Battling Choices

Yotam Gadot

Senior Editors & Producers: ContentoNow
Translator: Hagit Migron
Editor: Barry Rosenfeld
Cover Design: Benjie Herskowitz
Book Design: Talma Asher

ISBN: 978–965–550–550–4

International sole distributor: ContentoNow
22 Isserles Street, 6701457 Tel Aviv, Israel
www.ContentoNow.com
netanel@contentonow.com

Battling Choices

Yotam Gadot

It was on a sunny day in London, of all places, that She told me I needed to express myself because expressing myself would reveal my contradictions, and confronting the contradictions would lead me to an inner understanding.

Loyal to Wittgenstein as I was, what could not be spoken about, I was careful to pass over in silence.

GRABBING THE BULL BY THE HORNS
OF THE DILEMMA

> *A dilemma is not a situation where considerations*
> *merely clash, but one in which these considerations*
> *weigh heavily on the heart of the agent and threaten*
> *to paralyze him. He or she experiences feelings of*
> *helplessness and indecisiveness in the face of the*
> *situation.*
>
> (Dr. Danny Statman)

"Leather bag!"[1] – first alert.

"Leather bag!" – second alert.

Operations officer, Shahar, sounds the alert over the battalion network, as the other networks echo his call. The alarm is well underway as the men jump into their vehicles. As I reach my jeep, Hamid the driver arrives, and we are on our way. The radio is bursting with chatter. I try both the brigade network

---

1   IDF code word for infiltration or attack by an unknown aircraft.

and the battalion network. Shahar is trying to make sense of the incoming messages. The forward garrisons are just beginning to report.

"Kadim 3, this is Kadim 6. Report your status? Over."
"This is Kadim 3. Kadim 41 is on his way. Kadim 1 is in zone 9. Kadim 4 and Kadim 42 will be advancing in a minute."
Over the brigade network:
"This is Kadim. I'm taking zones 200 and 400, and zones 9 and 1."
"Kadim 41, this is Kadim 6. Zone 200 is yours. Kadim 3, this is Kadim 6. Tell Kadim 31 to take the northern roadblock and Kadim 2 can take the southern one. Go take up your positions.
"This is Kadim 3. Roger."
"Kadim 5, what is your position?"
"This is Kadim 5, on my way to zone 11."
"This is Kadim 6. Make sure Kadim 4 and 42 are on the way. Out."

Shachar, the ordnance officer, arrives at zone 200. Yigar reaches the Beit Hillel position and Shahar, the brigade operations officer, starts up his tank and is on the move. There's a sudden burst of gunfire! The network is jammed with messages. Shachar manages to break through and reports a sighting.
"Kadim stations, this is Kadim 6. Maintain radio silence! Kadim 41, this is Kadim 6. What is your status report? Over.
"This is Kadim 41. I think I see something!"
"This is Kadim 6. I'm on my way."

Operations officer, Shahar, reaches the hill and begins to scope the area.
"Kadim 6, this is Kadim 3. Object spotted at area 11, moving north to south."

"This is Kadim 6. Maintain visual contact. I'll be with you in a minute. Arriving from the north. State your position... This is Kadim 6, I have a visual on you. Out."

Over the brigade communication network, the brigade commander is requesting and comparing reports. The forces in the field are on the alert, watching for the slightest movement. Something as innocuous as a flight of birds can appear on the radar as a glider. Finally, the brigade operations officer announces, "One hour since start of incident." It seems like only minutes. After what feels like only a few more minutes, I look at my watch, and note, in reality three more hours have passed. It is 04:00 a.m. The brigade commander calls us in for a meeting.

We're back to "normal", I think. Back to the task of preparing the convoys and dispatching them to the military garrisons.[2] Today is a "convoy day". Following the briefing, I start to recall the forces back to the battalion base. Ilan, the company headquarters deputy commander, awaits them at the gate, making sure each man has unloaded his weapon.

One hour later, I'm back with the command group. At company headquarters everyone is busy, loading the command car and unloading the jeep, and mostly milling around, which is usual on the morning of a convoy day. Shahar already is waiting for me at the office, as impatient as always. I sit down slowly, to

---

2   Between 1985 and 2000, the Israeli army was deployed in a security belt, three to twelve kilometers wide, in South Lebanon, along the Israeli border. The purpose of this belt was to maintain a barrier between the Israeli population near the border and the terrorists present in South Lebanon. Convoys were periodically sent into this belt (known as the security zone) to resupply the Israeli garrisons.

buy time before he asks me the question. Shahar politely waits for me to sit down, and then asks, "Do we send in the convoys or not?" I reply, "How about a cup of coffee?"

By 08:00, the convoys are ready – two convoys and a command group. One convoy is to head for the Beaufort and Dlaat outposts and the second for Kawkaba. I should already be on my way out to inspect them, to make sure they are prepared.

But I wait another moment, staring into the depths of the dilemma, trying to see as far as my mental powers will take me. As always, time is against me. It seems the more I need of it, the less I have.

I look out the window through the morning mist to see Shahar heading toward the office. I know that my time is up. We must go out to inspect the logistics convoys, which will seek out improvised explosives (IEDs) and possible snipers along the supply route. There's no time for a thorough review, so I settle on a brief inspection of the soldiers' appearance. They appear well-groomed and prepared, having just completed a prior uniform inspection. After asking them a few questions to assess their level of concentration, I give Ido, the battalion communications officer, and Yaron, the deputy commander, the go ahead to get moving. Ido will head the Beaufort convoy and Yaron the Kawkaba convoy. All is ready. I authorize Hamid to commence and inform Shahar over the radio that the convoys are on the move. On the radio, I hear Ido giving the code-word, "Belgium", and Yaron the code-word, "Hagar." It's going well, I tell myself, and have no idea what is in store for me.

Ido crosses the Litani and begins climbing towards the ridge. The vehicles are moving quite slowly, keeping an even distance between them – not too small, so if a car-bomb arrives only one vehicle will be hit, and not too large, so they can assist one another in both observation and firepower. All eyes keep a constant watch on the sides of the road, trying to guess where trouble might come from. It can spring from any corner and lurks behind every bend, especially on this winding road.

Suddenly, from behind a bend a fast-moving Mercedes appears, picking up speed as it approaches the convoy. My first thought is – "a car-bomb". Ido, traveling in the first vehicle, signals for it to stop. The only visible reaction is increased acceleration. Before Ido can react, the Mercedes zooms past him. The commander in the following vehicle, a platoon sergeant from Tzafrir's company, fires in the air, the next signal to stop. The reaction of the Mercedes is the same: it accelerates some more. The soldiers in the third vehicle kneel and shoot to hit. And hit they do, well-trained soldiers that they are.

— The car stops abruptly.

It turns out that its passengers are not terrorists – in the car are General Lahad[3] and his aides!

Yaron, the battalion deputy commander, who heads the Kawkaba convoy, has already passed Marj-Ayoun and is almost at the UN checkpoint when a burst of gunfire slices through the air. The convoy comes to a halt. The gunfire carries with it the smell of failure, an acrid smell that reaches as far as my nostrils as well.

---

3   Commander of the South Lebanon Army, which was cooperating with the IDF at the time.

The dilemma:

To send in the logistics convoys or not?!

Alone in the office (Shahar has already left) I try to consider all of the facts. I know that the men of company headquarters have been on their feet for over 24 hours. I also know what the soldiers in the outposts are going through, how isolated they must feel. I know that we are their only link to the rest of the world.

I'm stuck.

It's a familiar feeling: the feeling of no way out or, alternatively, of too many options, with no way to choose among them all. In moments like these I envy scientists. When they are faced with a seemingly unsolvable predicament, they have one basic advantage. They can put the problem aside and return to it later. They can ponder it throughout the day or night, in whatever place they might find themselves. But I am in the here and now, and in the here and now I must find a solution - even if my mind isn't all that clear – even if I am tired. Even if my body is aching and limiting my ability to think.

Leibniz writes of a hungry donkey that stood between two piles of hay. Unable to decide which one to choose, he stayed in one place and died. Leibniz would have probably said to me, "The most important thing is that you decide."
"Is that more important than what I decide?!" I would hurl back at him.
"Indeed, coming to a decision is more important than the content of the decision. For by the act of deciding, you fulfill your duty to your soldiers and to the civilians living in the north of Israel."

His words only increase my distress, so I ask, "But how shall I decide, with what tools?" "This question has already been answered by the Greeks," he explains. "Let me tell you a story. Eulathus, who was greatly impressed with the Sophists' ability to win their trials, wished to learn their methods. He went to the Sophist Protagoras and said, 'Teach me.' The latter replied, 'The tuition fee is thus and such.' Eulathus said, 'Agreed. I shall pay you half now and half after winning my first trial.' They shook on it. After completing his studies, Eulathus did not practice the profession, and so did not win a trial and did not pay the second half of his tuition. Seeing that his pupil was not practicing law, Protagoras said to him, 'I shall sue you and then you will have to pay me. For if you lose, you will be obliged to pay me according to the court's ruling, and if you win, you will be obliged to pay me according to the agreement between us.' Eulathus replied, 'In either case I shall *not* have to pay you. For if I lose, I will be absolved from payment according to the agreement between us, and if I win, I will be absolved from payment by the ruling of the court.'"

Therefore, we have a conundrum. They are both right, and the issue cannot be decided.

"But what I learn from this case," Leibniz adds, is that you must choose a guiding principle, and base your decision upon it. Had Protagoras and Eulathus decided in advance that their agreement would override a court decision – or vice versa – this problem would not have arisen. So, I advise you to choose a guiding principle and make your decision accordingly."

I choose a principle: Preserving lives. As a supreme value, perhaps it will lead me to the solution. I feel glad to be making some progress; I am no longer stuck where I was five minutes ago.

I begin to proceed along the first branch of the fork, the "yes" branch – and see myself confronted by Tzafrir, the commander of the Beaufort and Dlaat outposts. I imagine what he would say to me: "The sense of isolation at the outposts is intense, even oppressive. Each outpost houses 25 to 50 soldiers, some of them infantrymen and some tank crew. Different individuals from different backgrounds with diverse values and beliefs. The overall situation – the many combat missions – by itself is both demanding and stressful. Since the number of missions is a function of the number of soldiers at the outpost, the garrison as a whole is only as strong as its weakest soldier. If we push that soldier past his breaking point, the system as a whole will break down. This weakest link is like an electrical fuse. The hard work by day, accompanied by the enemy ambushes at night, represents the total amount of stress that the garrison can legitimately handle. Any additional cause for stress is completely unjustifiable, both practically and morally. A convoy that doesn't arrive, or arrives without all the necessary materials, only increases the pressure. Any increased pressure diminishes the performance of the soldiers, and their level of performance is what ultimately determines whether a terrorist unit will succeed to infiltrate the Israel-Lebanon border or to operate against the Israeli forces within the South Lebanon security belt. We must see to it that the soldiers' performance does not falter, and must therefore guarantee that the soldiers at the forward bases are in the best possible shape at all times.

"So, if human lives are truly your priority, then you must put pressure on company headquarters general staff , and send in the supplies when they are needed!" – Tzafrir would say...

The "no" branch is represented in my mind by Yaron, the battalion deputy-commander. "Company headquarters has been on its feet and functioning continuously for over 24 hours," he would say. "Its abilities are compromised in many ways: Its alertness is diminished; nerves are frayed and patience and tolerance are at a low. There are other things to consider as well, but I am setting them aside for now. I am sticking to the guiding principle – the preservation of lives. From that perspective, it is the fatigue that worries me, the inability to maintain a high level of concentration, and our inability, as commanders, to sustain the necessary level of alertness. Consider the mountainous roads leading to Kawkaba and Beaufort. If just one driver falls asleep for even a second, we will pay for it in lives. If we run into the enemy while the soldiers aren't able to keep a high level of alertness, we will pay for it dearly. So if lives are your priority, your only choice is to cancel the convoys and let the men get a few hours of sleep."

The conundrum remains unresolved. The guiding principle has led me to contradictory conclusions. I start to feel mounting anxiety. I only hope Shahar doesn't walk in right now. If only I had some formula, some Pythagoras's theorem in which I could set the variables and work out a solution. But I do not have one. If only I had someone to consult – but I do not. So I ask myself, "How about a cup of coffee?"

To my aid comes Yaya (Maj. General Yoram Yair), who advises me to use the "expected value" theory. He tells me about a dilemma he faced: "I once had to make a very difficult decision," he tells me. "We were clearing mines and it was getting dark. Continuing the task would have exposed the men to great danger, but stopping for the night would have been very dangerous, too. I had to choose between the risk of letting them handle the mines and the booby traps in the dark and the risk of leaving a unit isolated behind a minefield... It was a choice between two evils. There was no safe way out and no option that did not involve considerable danger. In such a situation you must assess which option is more risky and how likely it is to materialize" (Yoram Yair, *With me from Lebanon*, p. 74).

He, Yaya, might possibly say to me, "There's a warning about a car bomb. The probability of this danger materializing is the greater." "True, this scenario is more likely to materialize," I would reply, "but the possibility of terrorists infiltrating the border always exists. And while I have the moral right to risk the lives of my men, I do not have the right to do anything that would endanger the lives of civilians, even remotely."

"Am I afraid of Pascal?" I ask myself. Pascal developed the principle of expected value to meet the needs of gamblers. Today, it is utilized in decision-making models, but in those models the gain and risk can be measured more or less accurately. But how can I use a formula that requires me to place a value on human life and then multiply it by some number? (The value will always be the same: Infinity).

And even if this value could be measured, would my situation be any better?! A short journey through the convoluted pathways of probability shows that the answer is – no.
The basic facts of this journey are two, but they can branch out indefinitely:
   A commander can make the right decision and fail in his mission;
   A commander can make the wrong decision and succeed in his mission.

The problem can be illustrated by the example of the unfair coin: A coin which lands 80 percent of the time on heads and only 20 percent of the time on tails. A rational man asking to bet on this coin would always bet on heads, because, if the coin behaves "correctly", he will lose only 20 percent of the time. But a gambler betting on this coin ten times in a row might still guess wrong each and every time. And yet, faced with the same dilemma again – heads or tails – he would again be compelled to choose heads. (As an aside, this might be the place to quote Napoleon's remark that generals need not only talent but also luck.) My point is that any decision model based on expected value – or on any other statistical parameter – is based on choosing the lesser evil, and as such it is first of all evil.

After realizing the distortions of the statistical approach, I was bothered by the question: Is there no better option? Can my position not be better than that of the gambler? Also, I have a recurring nightmare in which I face a bereaved mother and tell her, "On average, your son was not killed!"

The mathematicians also offer me the Minimax model. They suggest that I assess the maximum damage associated with each possible course of action, and choose the option in which the maximum damage is the least. "Using this model," I retort, "I would never be able to cross the road, since the maximum damage associated with crossing a road is getting killed, while the maximum damage associated with not crossing it is not going to work, not going to the store, or not going to a movie. No damage can be greater than losing my life. So what does that mean? That I must spend my life sitting at home?"

She dismisses my assertions with a wave of her hand and shoots out a single word: "Demagogy". I think She is right, but that I am right, too. So I say, "True, but beyond the absurdities it generates, the problem with this model is that it rules out any possibility of bold action (I believe there is no need to explain the importance of boldness in military history or history in general). Such action always involves great risk that can lead to considerable damage, and there is always an alternative that involves a smaller risk and less damage. Seeing in her eyes that I have failed to convince her, I pull out the last arrow in my quiver, saying, "Let's examine our dilemma by the light of this model."

Applying this model we find ourselves unable to choose between the options, for we cannot judge which is the lesser of the two maximum risks. The maximum harm that can result from not sending in the convoys is a terrorist infiltration, while the maximum harm that can result from sending them in is a car bomb attack on a convoy. The discussion of expected value outcomes above already showed that I have no way of choosing between these two options. And as an aside, let me point out that a football team playing according to the Minimax model would always get a score of 0:0, at the most.

Confused by the models and running out of time, I try to put my head... the battalion... in order.

The distress I am experiencing saps me of all of my powers of concentration. The last person I need to see right now is the Staff Sargent, but he picks this moment to walk in and mumble something. Maybe I should give him some positive feedback. But how? How can I? How can I give him positive feedback when I myself am in the pits of despair? "That's the source of my loneliness," I told her one Saturday, "the fact that I am never alone, not even for a moment. I don't have a single moment to myself, a quiet moment to sit and think. That's why I lack the strength to break through the dilemma and solve it." "That's not loneliness," She answered, and continued to hone her psychological analysis of my situation. But for me, I only want to solve the problem. I want to find some clue that will lead me to the solution. I want the Staff Sargent to leave already. And the time? It continues to advance as usual, moving slowly like a ponderous elephant, heavily, monotonously, as though it knows where it is going, as though it has some destination far beyond the horizon. But in the meantime, the men outside are loading the vehicles and preparing the convoys.

I begin to sense the time as a trap closing in on me. I am approaching the point where any decision I make, even the correct one, will probably be bad. In the words of renowned American automobile executive, Lee Iacocca, "Even the right decision is wrong if it comes too late." Iacocca stresses that every decision has a time frame in which it must be made, in order to be a good one, and it is better to make a calculated risk before the time is up than to hesitate too long. I would go even further and say that it is better to make a bad decision within the right timing than a good decision at the wrong timing. Mostly because the mere act of deciding clears up the fog of uncertainty and thus prevents the numerous adverse effects that uncertainty can cause. Iacocca would have said "decide now." Uncertainty is indeed the reason that Shahar, the operations officer, is standing in the doorway to my office. The expression on his face and his questioning look tell me that my time is up. Gathering all my strength, I say, "Shahar, tell Ilan to come in for a briefing, and in the meantime see about opening up all the routes. We are sending in the convoys."

The wisdom of the heart

Intuition: the wisdom of the heart, inspiration, unmediated knowledge, penetrating the essence of things by insight: "Man's internal world is largely composed of the inward gaze, of intuition, what the Jews call the holy spirit" (Joseph Klausner, Judaism, Vol. 1, 151, cited in the Even Shushan Hebrew Dictionary).

Ending A

The story is not yet over. I made a decision, but now I had to face her – She who had witnessed all my agony – and explain my decision and my reasons for it (which was often twice as hard as making the decision itself). She asked me how I eventually came to my decision.

"By intuition," I replied.

She: "What is intuition?"

Me: "I do not know."

She: "Describe the moment you came to the decision or the path that led you to it."

Me: "Two people guided me on my difficult path. Each of them in his way gave me the legitimacy to make the decision I felt had to be made. The first was Einstein. His address on deducing the laws of science lighted my path to making my decision. He said, "There is no logical path to these laws; only intuition, resting on sympathetic understanding of experience, can reach them." The second was Eyal, one of the battalion company commanders. He told me that, one Saturday, when he was at home on a weekend leave, he sensed something had happened in the company. He told his girlfriend about it and called the company. It turned out something had indeed happened: A command car had turned over.

The "intuition" evoked by Einstein is a profound mental perceptiveness, more powerful and more far-reaching than any analytic tool. I shall term this kind of intuition "supra-mental understanding." The sense of which Eyal spoke, by which we can perceive events that are far from us in place and time, the sense by which human perception can span great distances, or see into the past or the future, I shall term "supra-sensory perception."[4]

Intuition, I believe, is a combination of supra-mental understanding and supra-sensory perception. It is the combination of these forces that helped me crack the dilemma.

She: "Can you prove this?"

Me: "No, I cannot." Feeling defensive, I attack her unjustly and say: "But that is no reason to reject my claims. It may be a reason to exclude them from the realm of science, but that will not bother me, for many well-known fields of knowledge were criticized as "unscientific" for many years... And anyway, if reality is not scientific I prefer reality over science."

Seeing me getting excited and straying from the topic, She retorts: "If things are that simple, why the tendency to resort to mathematical models and computer programs?"

---

4   I prefer the terms *supra*-mental and *supra*-sensory to *extramental* and extrasensory, because the former terms better covey that intuition is contiguous to straightforward mental and sensory perception; they are all part of the same continuum.

"For the same reason that the man who lost his key looked for it under the lamppost," I say. "Mathematical models are notions we can understand, while supra-mental understanding and supra-sensory perception are beyond our grasp. People resort to mathematical models because they give them a sense of comprehension and confidence. Whereas my proposal, which stresses the importance of intuition, seems to say: "Take a leap into the unknown, into confusion, and what you will find there will be better than what the most sophisticated model can provide."

I wished to add two arguments that I had prepared, which take two different directions. First, that science would reject my claims just as it rejects parapsychology, and therefore I had suppressed these thoughts for several years. Fear of reactions like "prove it!" or "can you repeat the experiment?" paralyzed me. But now that I had resolved to be faithful to reality, I was confident of my description. It is an accurate reflection of reality.

The second argument takes me into the realm of science fiction. I painted her a picture of a battalion commander 30 years from now riding a tank – perhaps our son, if we have a son and he grows up to be a battalion commander. On his right, where the commander's machinegun is mounted today, there will be a small computer, or some other decision-aiding device. The commander will input the variables of the battlefield, and the machine will output the decisions he must make. Will this commander's decisions be better than mine? I am sorry to say that I am sure of my opinion: His decisions will be no better than ours, perhaps not even as good as ours. One reason is that the computer's solutions will depend on the parameters built into it by its programmers. Any program will need to define notions like "troop cohesion" or "mental fortitude," and assign them a weight in the decision-making processes. Thus, any such program will skew the results. But that is a secondary reason. The primary reason is that the computer is not able to sense the soldiers as the commander can using his supra-sensory perception. It will never know when they are nearing their breaking point, or when they need a two-minute rest, not because it is necessary for tactical reasons but because of what they are experiencing. Also, the computer will never have a holistic perception of the system called a battalion; it will never be able to see it as a whole that is much more than the sum of its parts.

And since I know that this computerized tank may well be the face of the future, I say today – perhaps in time and perhaps too late – that the machine has risen up against its maker. Trying to optimize our use of computers, we lose sight of the fact that computers lack abilities that are crucial on the battlefield. I do believe we should continue developing our computers and our analytical thinking (for reasons I will detail in the next chapters). But I also believe that it is more important to study intuition, in order to understand how to acquire it and how to use it to the best advantage.

We have come full circle, in a way. Now we face the dilemma of which branch of the fork to choose: the computer branch or the human branch. I suggest placing greater importance on the human factor, for it is men who do the fighting, today and in the future. Perhaps when we have battalions of robots, the computer will be a much more effective commander.

Though I cannot say much about intuition, I can point to the first step that needs to be taken. The first step is rooted in what is common to supra-mental understanding and to supra-sensory perception – and that is **love**.

A commander's love for his troops is a necessary condition for supra-sensory perception.

A commander's love for his profession is a necessary condition for supra-mental understanding.

Hence, a commander who does not love his unit and his profession can never be a good commander.

I am well aware that this assertion lacks the caution and responsibility required of a scientific assertion. But I believe that it has the honesty and emotional depth of an artistic statement. And I hope that this advantage, weighed against the cost, ultimately yields a better decision-making process.

She: "So how did the story end?"

Me: "The shots heard in the vicinity of Yaron's convoy were fired by UN troops that were training in the area. Ido's convoy accomplished its mission, but at a greater cost. General Lahad was not hurt, but the event had its repercussions. The brigadier general and the division commander arranged a meeting with him to let everyone blow off some steam (in the meeting he admitted he had been driving recklessly, by the way), and I got a reprimand from the division commander. But there was no terrorist infiltration."

A commander makes decisions using his intuition.
By the term intuition I mean supra-mental
understanding and supra-sensory perception.

Anyone relying on various mathematical models
to solve the decision-making problem or to optimize
decision-making processes is like the man who looked
for his lost key under the lamppost.
We must focus on the concept of intuition and try to
understand it and optimize it.

Ending B

The story is not yet over. I made a decision, but now I had to face her – She who had witnessed all my agony – and explain my decision and my reasons for it (which was often twice as hard as making the decision itself). She asked me how I eventually came to my decision.

"By intuition," I replied.

She: "What is intuition?"

Me: "I do not know... but I know what its yields are."

"What are they?"

"Its yields are anything a man knows which enters his consciousness not through his five senses and not through logical reasoning, whether deductive or inductive.

"How did you arrive at this idea?"

"Two people guided me on my path. Each of them in his way gave me the legitimacy to make the decision I felt had to be made. The first was Einstein. His address on deducing the laws of science lighted my way to making my decision. He said: "There is no logical path to these laws; only intuition, resting on sympathetic understanding of experience, can reach them." The second was Eyal, one of the battalion company commanders. He told me that, one Saturday, when he was at home on weekend leave, he sensed that something had happened in the company. He told his girlfriend about it and called the company. It turned out something had indeed happened: A command car had turned over. Einstein spoke of intuition as bypassing all logical reasoning and arriving directly at the truth. Eyal described it as bypassing all our senses and, again, arriving directly at the truth.

"I understand what you are saying, but I do not understand how, of all the objects of your awareness, you choose one and know that it is correct. To put it simply, how did you know that the correct choice was to send in the logistics convoys?"

"I know the physical feeling that accompanies intuitive knowledge. It is a sense of certainty, a feeling of comfort and calm that spreads through my body. I experience a sense of inner completeness. This feeling comes when intuition gives me a *positive* directive, as in the case of the convoys. There is a different feeling that comes with a *negative* directive, namely with an intuitive sense of danger that serves as a warning bell. In that case the feeling is one of mental disquiet, a sense of conflict that induces frustration – frustration that grows the longer I fail to identify its source."

She asked me many questions that day, and I had answers only to a few. But I felt good about these answers, I felt they were leading me to where I am today. For example, She asked: "What do you mean by 'sympathetic understanding'... 'reaching the truth'…? I replied from my own experience (and what I said is true only for me, and only from certain perspectives). "When I first noticed the presence of intuition," I said, "I was passive with regards to it. When it appeared, I used it, and when it failed to appear, I used the analytic tools that were then available to me. But since then I have grown more aware. I have improved my ability to access intuitive knowledge. I can now trigger it at will. The improvement in my technique coincided with the improvement in my ability to recognize intuition.

A problem I faced was telling the difference between genuine intuitive judgment and judgment based on raw emotion – namely what I wanted to happen, or what I feared. When my intuition seemed to point me in the direction I wanted to take in the first place, or, alternatively, seemed to rule out an option that frightened me, I could not be sure that it was not simply my desire speaking, or my fear. The error was an error of commission: I identified judgments as intuitive when they did not in fact arise by intuition. To solve this problem, I trained myself to recognize the feeling triggered by true intuition: the sense of calm associated with a positive judgment and the feeling of disquiet associated with a negative one.

At this point I identified another problem, this one an error of omission. I realized that, while deliberating what to do, I tended to consider *only* the possibilities in which I had an emotional stake, namely those I either feared or desired, and to ignore other possibilities. To avoid this I trained myself to consider all practical courses of action, and examine each of them by the light of intuition.

Only after effectively perfecting these skills did I dare to advance further by trying to actively *trigger* intuitive knowledge. At this point I could be fairly confident of my judgment.

She also asked me, "Is there any necessary condition for the appearance of intuition or for triggering it?" "Yes," I replied. "Though it is important to distinguish between intuition and emotion, it is nevertheless crucial to have an emotional attachment to the scenario in question, or to the people involved in it.

"I deem this emotional attachment very important, for several reasons. First, it is the upper threshold that determines one's access to intuition. A person with high emotional abilities has better access to intuitive knowledge. Second – and this has general implications for our culture – we must understand that we are dealing with a channel of knowledge that can be highly effective. This effectiveness can never be achieved by technological means, no matter how advanced, since these technologies have no emotional dimension. I mean to say that the communication between a commander and his unit can improve in ways we do not even consider. This communication is anchored in a different plane of reality, which may yield better results than information provided by computers."

Her last question was: "Why didn't you speak of this to your subordinates?" I laughed. "I was afraid," I said, "simply afraid that they would think I was crazy, or that I had begun to dabble in the occult. So I sufficed with encouraging them to relate to their units on an emotional level; this is something I greatly emphasized. I tried, in various ways, to enhance their sense of affection and sympathy for their men, just as I did for myself. If I had to do it all over again today, I would do the same thing.

I would avoid sharing all my ideas, since I don't think there is sufficient openness yet to deal with the issues I have raised here."

She: "So how did the story end?"

Me: "The shots heard in the vicinity of Yaron's convoy were fired by UN troops that were training in the area. His convoy accomplished its mission. Ido's convoy accomplished its mission too, but at a greater cost. General Lahad was not hurt, but the event had its repercussions. The brigadier general and the division commander arranged a meeting with him to let everyone blow off some steam (in the meeting he admitted he had been driving recklessly, by the way), and I got a reprimand from the division commander. But there was no terrorist infiltration."

**There are three paths by which one may
attain knowledge:
1. The senses   2. Logical inference   3. Intuition
Where we cannot utilize the first two, it behooves us to
utilize the third;
Where we can utilize one or both of the first two, it is
still advisable to utilize the third as well, in order to gain
complementary knowledge.**

PATHS OF WAR (DECISIONS)[5]

Once, during a visit to the Command and Staff College, I heard an interesting story,
namely that in one of the staff-meetings in the German army, all the participants opted – independently – for the same course of action. The claim was made by the head instructor, and his goal in mentioning it was to make two points:

1. On the battlefield, there is always one solution that is best.
2. The German army had reached such a high level of professionalism that all its officers were adept in employing the reasoning that would lead them to this solution.

I pointed out to him that a battlefield is an arena with two players, and introduced him to the paradox of the best plan.

---

5 This chapter is informed by Karl Popper's theory of scientific method, whose main principles are freedom of thought and logical falsifiability.

The paradox of the best plan (or the paradox of surprise)

If, in assessing situations, we employ a model of reasoning that consistently yields the same good plan – and it is immaterial if it is the only good plan or the best plan of several – and this plan is the one chosen, then no matter how much we enhance our war principles with the principle of strategy, we will never achieve the element of surprise. This is because by learning our method of reasoning, the enemy will always be able to anticipate our actions. And given the obvious fact that attaining surprise is a crucial factor in any good military plan, it follows that we will never achieve good planning. The conclusion I drew from this paradox, I said, is that "there is not, and must not be, one best course of action that is always chosen in a given battle situation."

At this point in the conversation, the head instructor turned his back on me and left. At first I did not understand his behavior, but after recovering from the shock of his sudden departure, I realized that it had probably stemmed from confusion. I do not think it was a personal fault of his alone that led him to believe in the existence of a single best plan. The problem, I believe, is cultural; all of us, members of Western society, suffer from it. A culture based upon the law of non-contradiction can never allow itself more than one best solution. My complaint is not against the instructor, but against the system – the system that demands order and a scale of optimality because this is the only language it understands.

Now I suddenly understood her claim about the contradictions, the claim She had been making since we met, that "only a person who accepts the contradictions within him can live a better and more complete life". I understood that the officer who accepts contradictions, instead of trying to eliminate them, and who embraces confusion and finds within it the good and the beautiful, is the one who will formulate the best plans.

Confusion is what alarmed the head instructor, it is what every member of our Western culture finds dangerous and disturbing – and not altogether without reason. Order is the mainstay of civilization; it is what makes it possible for us to go to the grocery store and buy bread. But for me, this conversation was the final nail in the coffin of what is known as the estimate of the situation model. It was at this moment that I discarded that model for good.

The journey began at a different moment, in a different landscape and especially with different people. It began with General Amiram Levin at the Beaufort outpost, near the ancient Beaufort castle.

There is something intimidating about the climb up to the Beaufort garrison. The castle looms large and tall, well-suited to the rugged landscape. But that was not the reason for my excitement every time I visited the place. The reason was the way the castle suddenly appeared right out of the Litani cliffs. Every time I came there I would ask myself the same question: Where does God's handiwork end and man's begin? On the way there I could never stop thinking long enough to focus my thoughts on finding the answer. I was always preoccupied with the problems and the tasks of the day ahead. On the way back, with the day's work completed, I could then concentrate and set my mind on the matter, and only then would I try to solve the riddle. But by then it would usually be dusk, with the sun sinking low behind the castle, sending its rays through the cracks in its walls (usually directly into my eyes) and I could never discern the exact point at which the masonry met the bedrock. I always promised myself that on my next trip, I would find the solution. But it never happened.

Nor was I thinking about the matter on this particular trip with General Amiram Levin. I was preoccupied with the usual question that always occupied my thoughts before any meeting between the soldiers and generals: which idiot would throw out some silly remark that would start a commotion we wouldn't be able to stop, no matter how much energy we devoted to it? (That energy is already as good as wasted, I thought, but I will have to waste it anyway, if only to keep the system running smoothly).

But the surprise this time was that nobody said anything stupid, and I was starting to think we would be able to concentrate on the essentials, when General Levin noticed a Golani soldier with a tear in his shoe, and the usual song-and-dance began.[6] Levin asks the soldier if they don't replace worn out shoes at this outpost, the soldier answers whatever he answers. The exchange between them is not important, it is secondary. The real conversation takes place with the eyes: General Levin looks at me, I look at Tzafrir, the company commander, Tzafrir looks at the platoon commander, and so on, until the circle completes itself and a new round of glances begins. All the looks convey the same message: it'll be ok, we'll take care of it.

Why am I telling all this? Why am I heaping on irrelevant details? Only to show that it was just another day until the bombshell was dropped. After Levin ended the talk, he went

---

6   Golani is an elite infantry brigade that is often tasked with the toughest missions; however, it is also known for discipline problems.

up to the observation point and corrected his map to conform with the terrain. I stayed behind a bit talking to Tzafrir, and then followed him. When I reached the observation post, he asked me for the details of the post's "Hannibal Plan" (a plan of action in case of a kidnapping). I presented the main considerations and explained the plan. General Levin asked a couple of questions, thought for a couple minutes, and then suggested a plan of his own.

Before he even finished presenting it, I could see that it was superior to our own, and this bothered me. We had put in several hours of deliberation and obtained the approval of the brigade commander, but Levin, after two minutes on the rock at the observation post, had come up with a better plan. After presenting his plan, he looked me in the eye, and I did not know what to say. I thought of saying "how about a cup of coffee", but held my tongue.

On the way back, the question of the castle's convergence with the cliff could not have been farther from my thoughts. The realization of my inferior military planning – the fact that something was keeping me stuck at a mediocre level – drove everything else from my mind and dominated my thoughts. Again and again I reviewed the process by which I had come to my decision, and the more I thought about it the more concerned I became. On the one hand, I had devoted several hours to my plan, proceeding systematically (according to the Situation Estimate process). I had consulted the relevant staff officers (company commanders Ofer, Yigar, Tzafrir and Yaron) and obtained the approval of the brigade commander and the division commander. But General Levin, standing for two minutes on a rock at the Beaufort observation post, had come up with a better plan.

Yotam Gadot

That was only the beginning. Then came two battalion operations. The first was Operation Marbek carried out in the northern part of the South Lebanon Security Belt, conducted about one week after my visit to the Beaufort outpost. The details of the operation, as I recorded them later, were as follows:

1. Order of battle:
    a. Infantry force: 15 men led by Battalion 432 deputy commander.
    b. Force led by L Company commander Yigar:
        1. Engineering task force led by one officer.
        2. Bomb disposal team led by one officer.
        3. Two tanks.
        4. One armored personnel carrier (APC).
    c. Rescue and recovery force:
        1. Ordnance recovery team led by the battalion maintenance officer.
        2. Medical evacuation team led by the battalion doctor (on an APC).
        3. One tank.

2. The mission:
    a. Day observation and night ambush in the Marah Mubarak area.
    b. Clearing the route up to Marah Mubarak.

3. Timeline:
    a. 00:40 – Infantry force dispatched.
    b. 04:34 – Infantry force deployed at Marah Mubarak.
    c. 05:30 – L Company commander's force embarked.
    d. 07:05 – L Company commander's force identified first mine; bomb disposal team commenced removal of mine.

e. 08:15 – First mine detonated.
f. 08:35 – L Company commander's force identified second mine.
g. 09:00 – Second mine detonated.
h. 10:48 – Mine exploded under tank of L Company commander (Yigar).
i. 11:20 – Fourth anti-tank mine detonated by the bomb disposal team.
j. 15:15 – Battalion maintenance officer stepped on a mine.
k. 16:30 – Battalion maintenance officer evacuated.
l. 17:21 – Tank recovery commenced; APC ran over anti-personnel mine.

Let us join the operation at 10:48, just as Yigar's tank hit a mine. The background details relevant here are the composition of the lead force and its mode of operation. Foremost in the lead force were the engineers and the bomb disposal team, who cleared the route using mine prodders and minesweepers. Behind them came the APC, equipped with a mine roller,[7] and behind it came Yigar, the lead force commander, riding a tank that was also equipped with a mine roller.

At this point I was with the command group at the Kawkaba outpost. My vantage point was good, I could see the route almost from end to end. At 10:48 I saw a black mushroom of smoke rising from the area through which the lead force was moving. I called Yigar on the radio, and after a while he responded and reported that his tank had hit a mine. I asked him

---

7   A mine roller, or mine trawl, is a set of steel wheels mounted in front of a tank, designed to detonate anti-tank mines and thus to clear a lane through a minefield.

what the damage was, and he told me that the front suspension had been blown off. I instructed him to sweep the area around the tank for more mines, and in the meantime I considered the situation.

Yigar's tank was the fourth piece of gear to run over that particular mine. Before the tank passed, three other pieces of gear had passed over it – the APC's mine roller, the APC itself, and then the tank's own roller – without causing it to explode. Moreover, before they all passed we had swept the route with prodders and minesweepers, but did not locate it. Something here is acting very strangely, I thought. Later the demolitionists, also troubled by that question, would offer several possible explanations.

As I was considering various options, Yigar came over the radio and reported that the bomb disposal team had discovered yet another mine, a few meters in front of his tank (and behind the APC), and that they were preparing to detonate it. Following this, we had two tasks to perform: to continue clearing the route and to recover the tank. From the sound of Yigar's voice over the radio I knew that I had to get down there, to the place where his tank was stranded, and make my decision on the ground.

I boarded the APC with the ordnance and medical rescue teams, and we set out to join the lead force. When we arrived, I asked Yigar if they had finished sweeping the area around the tank with prodders and minesweepers, and he said that they had. Shaul the ordinance officer and I climbed down from the APC. We joined Yigar and went over to inspect the tank. We agreed that the track had to be reconnected so that the tank could be towed down the slope without needing another vehicle to support it from behind. To perform this we had to pull the tank backwards. I said to Yigar, "Come on, let's do this," and he asked, "How? To tow the tank backwards someone has to sit in the driver's seat, and the tank can't take another explosion like this. Its escape hatch has been blown off and its right hull is bent." He was right. If we drove the tank backwards it could hit another mine, and if this happened the driver would have no chance of surviving. We could check again with the prodder and the minesweeper, but we could not be sure whether there was another mine or not. More than that, we could not gauge the relative likelihood of this possibility.

After considering the various options, I was convinced that there was no choice but to pull the tank backwards. But I did not have it in me to order anyone to take the driver's seat, nor at first, did I have the courage to take it myself. But I knew I must not be seen to hesitate. In a situation like this, hesitation looks like helplessness. Eventually, I bit the bullet. I lowered myself into the driver's seat, and ordered Yigar to begin the towing operation. All went well. After pulling the tank backwards we approached it to take another look at the loose tread. Suddenly: BOOM. I was thrown backwards, and did not understand what had happened until I saw Hamtzani's leg. "Shit," I thought.

Then there was no time to think. We had to make sure that Hamtzani and the others received proper immediate medical attention, report back to our commanding officers, and perform many other tasks. But shortly afterwards, we had to decide how to proceed. And I had no idea if there were other mines, and if so, how many. I also knew the enemy was watching us and listening, and it was hard to assess what their next step would be. I did not know what to do; never before had I been in this situation. Military doctrine did not address this specific scenario. At that moment it dawned on me that not only did I not know what to do, I *could* not know! For some reason this calmed me and I began giving orders.

It was then that I realized the disadvantages of standard military thinking.

The third incident took place in the West Bank, in Jenin. The task we had to perform was neither simple nor entertaining: We had to impose a closure on one of the villages in the district and search it for wanted terrorists in collaboration with the Shabak (the state security agency). But the way we were issued our orders provided us with some amusement.

At 23:30, I reported to the brigade headquarters along with the operations officer, Ofer, and two company commanders, Eyal and Avishai, to receive our orders. The brigade commander was waiting for us in his office. He invited us in and started briefing us. "The operation starts in five hours," he said. We were surprised. Operation? What operation? But he ploughed ahead, pointing to a map, indicating the village and the routes leading to it. The map is some distance from us. We can't see a thing. An office girl comes in and says something to him. He answers her and continues the briefing. Suddenly – a power outage. We sit in the dark and wait. The operations officer fetches some candles, and the brigade commander continues by their feeble glow. The map is still far away from us, on the wall, and if previously we could barely see it, now we can barely see the commander. At this point, Avishai bursts out laughing. His laughter is catching. We sit there and laugh, unable to stop. The commander finally picks up the hint, and understands that we are not communicating. He stops for a moment and I ask the company commanders to leave. This is an improvement. We examine the map by candlelight and decide on the mission.

When I left his office, I collected the company commanders and we climbed into the jeep. I sat and tried to process all the details, using diagrams and a map, and to finalize the plan. It was already half past midnight. The commanders intervened and said that, if they didn't get their orders right away, they would not be able to stay on schedule. They were right. The constraints were simple: it would take us an hour to rejoin the company, and the company needed an hour to reach the vicinity of the village. Then half an hour for the briefing, and an hour to deploy around the village on foot. We also had to factor in a 30-minute margin for dealing with possible problems. But I was right too. The mission required me to learn many details before finalizing the plan. I had to learn the lay of the land and the routes of approach to the village, match the tasks to the various units, and attend to many other details. This is the crux of a commander's task: to assimilate a large amount of facts very quickly and issue decisive orders. The weight of information made me anxious, but ultimately the time consideration was more important. So I extracted the most pertinent information from the map and issued an order.

The Situation Estimate process

These three incidents prompted me to try to diagnose the essence of military questions, and to examine the process we use to solve these kinds of issues. To be honest, I originally identified a flaw in my own military thinking, and now I wanted to isolate the factors and determine whether the problem lay in me, or rather in the standard protocol of military planning that every IDF commander learns in officers' training school – the process known as the Commander's Estimate of the Situation. The obvious way to do this is to identify the characteristics of military problems, and then examine the Situation Estimate process by their light.

There are three characteristics of military issues:
1. There is never just one single solution.
2. There are always factors of uncertainty.
3. The information load is usually high (i.e., the ratio between the amount of data to be processed and the time available to process it).

The conclusion to be drawn from these characteristics is that, in dealing with a military problem, we must employ not only analytical thinking but also skills of associative (or intuitive) thinking – namely such skills as imagination, creativity, intuition, and holistic perception. Imagination and creativity are crucial because without them it is impossible to achieve an element of surprise. Intuition is useful in that it reduces the factor of uncertainty, and holistic perception allows one to assimilate large amounts of information at a glance and to categorize it correctly.

Having outlined the characteristics of the military problem and how they relate to the decision making process, I went on to analyze the Situation Estimate process itself. I began by examining the existing definitions of this term. Contemporary Israeli military literature offers two definitions:

1. The Estimate of the Situation is "a process of analyzing the factors that affect the accomplishment of a given mission, conducted based on the Principles of War and the War fighting

Doctrine, aimed at identifying the **course of action** that, according to these principles and this doctrine, constitutes the **best way to accomplish the mission**, given the existing constraints" (*Situation Estimate*, IDF Operations Department/ Instruction Division/War fighting Doctrine Branch, 1990, p. 1, emphases mine).

2. The Estimate of the Situation is "a given framework for a process of deliberation based upon **a logical and systematic process of studying and analyzing all the factors** that can affect the accomplishment of a mission, drawing conclusions, formulating possible courses of action, comparing them, minimizing their limitations and maximizing their advantages, and developing one chosen course of action." (*Battle Command and Procedure at the Battalion Level*, IDF Operations Department/Instruction Division/ War fighting Doctrine Branch, 1989, p. 23, emphases mine).

As these definitions show, the Situation Estimate process employed in the IDF today involves a series of consistent and logical steps aimed at learning and analyzing all the information relevant to the problem at hand and reaching a single solution. In other words, it is a systematic and consistent algorithm which involves proceeding from one step to the next. This process maximizes the use of "vertical" (analytical) thinking, but precludes the possibility of incorporating "horizontal" elements (such as imagination, creativity, etc). This, I believe, is its main drawback – and I shall establish this both theoretically and empirically. My theoretical argument is based upon an analysis of the process as it is described in the book *Situation Estimate*, from which the first definition is drawn. (See reference above).

The Situation Estimate process involves three broad stages:
1) the commander decides on a course of action;
2) the commander's plan is translated into operational terms;
3) the plan is put down in writing. Stages 2 and 3 are irrelevant to our discussion, because stage 3 is purely technical and stage 2, though it involves elements that are not technical, is essentially complementary to the commander's decision. Let us therefore focus on the first stage, in which the commander formulates possible courses of action and selects one of them. This stage is described in the book as follows:

> The commander's decision ("the stratagem")
> a. Diagnosis: the commander analyzes the operative factors (of the existing situation) based on the War fighting Doctrine and in light of "the mission" and "the aim," in order to identify the weak points of the enemy and identify the decisive point.
> b. Prognosis (course of action):
> Based on the War fighting Doctrine and the operative factors, and in light of the mission and the aim, the commander works out possible courses of action (COAs) – of our forces and of the enemy – assesses them, selects the chosen course of action (CCOA), and informs the staff of the CCOA."

A close examination of this excerpt, and of the Appendix to this chapter (see below), reveals that the Situation Estimate process is a systematic procedure that involves analyzing the important parameters of the battlefield (the terrain, the relative strength of the forces, considerations of time and space, and other factors); drawing conclusions in a systematic manner; processing the conclusions into possible courses of action (COAs), and choosing one (the CCOA). It is a process that proceeds from step to step in an analytical manner. According to this protocol, it is not legitimate to propose a course of action just because we imagined or intuited it; all action must derive from conclusions analytically deduced from the facts.

Karl Popper argues against this type of reasoning – though in a different context – in his paper "On The Sources of Knowledge and Ignorance":

> "The proper epistemological question is not one about sources; rather, we ask whether the assertion made is true – that is to say, whether it agrees with the facts, and we try to find this out, as well as we can, by examining or testing the assertion itself; either in a direct way, or by examining or testing its consequences."

That is, the fact that the possible course of action must be derived from the conclusions using a set of rigid rules and principles, precludes us from proposing ideas that are radical or unconventional.

When I presented this analysis to the doctrine experts in the IDF, they agreed with me that associative thinking plays an important role in solving military problems. But they disagreed that the Situation Estimate process, as employed in the IDF today, neutralizes this kind of thinking (I could have presented a simple counter-argument: the minute they assume the existence of a best solution they predetermine the character of the process and steer it in an analytic direction. But I opted for a harder yet more persuasive method).

To assess the validity of my claim – that the Situation Estimate process suppresses imaginative and original thinking – I conducted an experiment at the IDF Command and Staff College, where the IDF's high-ranking officers are trained (see Appendix 1 of this chapter for details of the experiment). The findings were that, after taking a standard course in Situation Estimate, students given an identical problem tended to propose an identical solution (to be precise, 16 out of 17 gave the exact same solution). When I presented this finding to one of the college instructors (not the instructor mentioned at the beginning of this chapter), he asked whether the plan they chose was a good one. When I replied that it was, he said, "Splendid, so the plan was good and all the students arrived at it!" The only thing he forgot was that, had the enemy been a graduate of the Command and Staff College, he could have anticipated this plan and easily foiled it. I told him I intended to entitle my study "Is the IDF Capable of Achieving Surprise at the Tactical Level?" and to use my findings to answer this question with a resounding "No!" As expected, he referred me to Barbara Tuchman's book *The Guns of August*, and to the example of the German officers who arrived independently at the very same plan – a plan that surprised the Russian general Samsonov.

I will take this opportunity to answer the three Command and Staff instructors, each of whom has also heard this from me in person: The Germans' big success, and the surprise they achieved, was made possible by one of two factors (choose whichever you prefer):

1. They got lucky.
2. Samsonov was unfamiliar with the German way of thinking (Had he been familiar with it, they wouldn't have managed to surprise him).

To phrase it more allegorically, my conclusion is as follows:

1. During the course, the students were all "programmed" to produce identical outputs.
2. Though they recognize the importance of associative thinking, the college instructors teach a method of thinking that suppresses it.

A commander using the standard Situation Estimate process will never – except in rare cases – come up with a brilliant plan, even if he possesses excellent skills and is highly aware of the importance of imagination. The reason is that his method of thinking shackles him, confining him to a limited range of mediocre ideas.

The impact of the "Principles of War" on the Situation Estimate process

Another domain I inspected for possible roots of mediocre planning was the Principles of War that are taught to IDF commanders. I examined these principles from the perspective of planning, in order to assess how they affect the courses of action we consider and the course of action we choose. Looking into this question, I noted that we first of all discern an entire set of principles that are irrelevant, namely: adherence to the mission in light of the aim; initiative and offensive action; depth and reserves; continuity of action and sustainability, and security. The first of these – adherence to the mission in light of the aim – should not be a principle of war; it should be a value that guides us in most spheres of life. It is just as relevant to business and education, for example, as it is to war. Hence, this value must be part of any course of action considered. The way to ensure this is for the military system to expel anyone who proposes courses of action that are incompatible with this value. Only thus will we effectively inculcate this desirable behavior.

A similar argument can be made for the principle of initiative and offensive action. A commander must understand that in every battle there is a sub-battle – a struggle for the initiative – and the side that wins this sub-battle has the best chances of winning the battle itself. Initiative is crucial because he who possesses it does not have to know the intentions of the enemy. And since the enemy's intentions are one of the factors that most crucially affect the quality of a commander's decision, seizing the initiative increases the probability of making good decisions. In other words, initiative moderates the effect of the uncertainty factor. Hence, initiative and offensive action must always be intrinsic components of a commander's behavior.

The same is also true for depth and reserves, continuity of action and sustainability, and security. These too are principles that a commander must always adopt in his behavior and thinking, and they too must be manifest in every conceivable course of action. Hence there is not much point in using them to assess possibilities.

Next comes a set of principles which, I believe, incline the commander's thinking towards the mediocre and must therefore be discarded. The first of these is logistical feasibility. In many Situation Estimates processes I observed, or in which I took part, a logistics officer came forward and told the commander what could be done. And that, of course, is a grave error. The task of the logistics officer is not to tell the commander what is logistically feasible, but rather to tailor a logistic solution to fit the commander's plan. Obviously, any plan will ultimately have to conform to logistical constraints. But if logistic considerations limit the plan in advance, the plan will inevitably be unimaginative. Consider the following scenario. Let's say that I, a battalion commander, must capture targets within the Syrians' outermost belt of defense. Unhampered by considerations of logistics, I might conceive the idea of flying the battalion directly to Tel Shams. But this idea will never be aired if I discard it in advance as impractical. Once such a plan is conceived, one of two things will happen. A thorough examination might lead to the conclusion that it is indeed impossible, in which case it will be shelved, even if from every other aspect it is brilliant. (This is what I mean when I speak of plans ultimately "conforming to logistical constraints"). Alternatively, the logistics officer, in a joint effort with the air force, may find a way to solve the problem – in which case the plan will be actualized, unlikely as it originally seemed. What I wish to stress here, as in the previous section, is the importance of not letting imaginativeness be stifled in advance by relying solely and exclusively on analytical thinking.

Another principle that produces the same effect is that of simplicity. Obviously, given two possibilities of equal merit, it makes sense to choose the simpler one. However, perceiving simplicity as a principle predisposes us to seek simple solutions, and diminishes our chances of conceiving ideas that are clever yet complex. In other words, a superior plan may be rejected just because it lacks simplicity.

Three other principles – optimal utilization of forces, concentration of efforts, and maintenance of morale and fighting spirit – all have to do with the management of forces, and I shall therefore reduce them into one principle by that name (On the importance of this reduction, see below). I am therefore left with two principles:

1. Stratagem (which includes surprise, deception, ploys, ruses).
2. Management of forces.

However, I am clearly still missing a factor that is crucial in any confrontation between two sides, namely the factor of relative advantage. A commander must always consider where his advantage over the enemy lies and how it can best be leveraged. This is a crucial criterion in assessing possible courses of action and choosing among them. I therefore add this principle to my list.

At the end of this process, I am left with three Principles of War:
1. Stratagem.
2. Seizing the relative advantage.
3. Management of forces.

Here, let me add that the limited number of principles is a great advantage in terms of people's ability to remember them, especially under stress. A survey I conducted found that most officers do not have a thorough knowledge of the Principles of War. The reasons for this could be two: Either the officers lack professionalism, or there is an essential problem with the principles themselves. Since I sampled a large number of officers, and am familiar with them and know they are not lazy, I was inclined to believe that the fault was not theirs. Nor did I believe that it lay in the way they were taught. Since the phenomenon is sweeping, I conclude that the problem does not lie solely in the men (either the officers or their instructors), but that another factor is at play – namely the nature of the principles themselves.

Searching for the flaw, the first thing I thought of was the large number of principles. I asked myself whether an officer, in circumstances of mental distress and limited time, could review all these principles in his mind – and concluded that he could not. I therefore set out to reduce the number of principles as far as possible by eliminating and combining some of them. The process of reduction has already been explained above. So now all that remains is to examine the new, concise, set of principles, and check how they affect the model of thinking that is meant to produce good decisions.

The **first and most important principle** is that of **stratagem**. It is crucial because it outweighs all the others. A plan that is superb in every aspect, but lacks the element of surprise, will be less effective than a bad plan that contains an element of surprise. To understand the importance of surprise, I set out to define it, and also to exemplify it using an effective analogy.

Definition: Surprising the enemy means making a maneuver that shatters his pattern of thought.

As for the analogy, the most fitting one, to my mind, is that of a chess game. This analogy is apt because there are many similarities but also many differences, and it is the differences, contrasted with the similarities, that shed light on the importance of surprise on the battlefield. Chess is a game of rules, whereas war is a game that has no rules, except for one: the rule that "anything goes." In chess, a white bishop will always be confined to the white squares, and a castle will always move in a straight line. In battle, as I said, anything goes. What does this mean? It means that, in war, one can take a white bishop and place it on a black square (or fly an armored battalion directly to Tel Shams), thereby delivering the enemy a decisive blow. This is why a computer can beat the greatest grandmaster of chess, but it will never outsmart a good general on the battlefield – and certainly not a brilliant one. A computer can be programmed with rules and possible moves, but cannot be programmed to do the unexpected. This is because any programming involves a pattern of thought or a set of rules, and on the battlefield the idea is to break the rules – not just break the direction of thought.

This explains why a battalion commander standing in the turret of a tank in the year 2020 will not make better decisions than mine if his only advantage over me is access to an advanced computer. Incidentally, the conclusion, from our perspective, is that in military thinking, the element of imagination must outweigh the element of analytical thinking – much more so than in chess.

The **second most important** principle is **seizing the relative advantage**. Its importance derives from the fact that, when surprise cannot be achieved, the effective use of relative advantage is likely to decide the battle. On the strategic level, it might be said that a battalion commander must always be sure to possess the advantage in fighting equipment.

The American victory in the 1991 Gulf War was achieved through the correct use of this principle, not through stratagem as is usually asserted. After delivering their opening blow, consisting of massive airstrikes, the Coalition forces did not require a significant surprise tactic to achieve victory. The surprise in this case only secured them a quicker and more decisive victory. Moreover, the surprise itself was achieved through the correct use of the relative advantage principle. Had it not been for their massive superiority in air power and electronics, the Americans could have never carried out their great outflanking maneuver without being discovered.

The relevant conclusion is that a commander should prefer those courses of action that maximize the principle of advantage.

In addressing the **third principle – management of forces –** let me highlight an issue that is often neglected through inattention or insensitivity, namely matching the mission to the force, no less than matching the force to the mission. In other words, never create a plan that is like a torture chamber for your troops; when you plan, remember who is meant to carry out the plan (this is similar to designing a new product, where the most important consideration is the identity of the "end user"). Notice that, heretofore, I generally warned against errors of omission, that is, rejecting in advance ideas that might be feasible. Here I warn against an error of commission: formulating a plan that the troops are unable to execute.

Returning to the larger issue of the Situation Estimate process, let me pause once again to concentrate on the distinction between errors of omission and errors of commission. As I said, we have been focusing on the former. We saw how the existing protocol can cause a commander to discard, or even fail to consider, possibilities that might be successful. But I disregarded errors of commission, namely the error of conceiving substandard plans. The reason I neglected this issue is that the analytic process, by its very nature, is immune to errors of this sort. Hence, in seeking an alternative process, we must find one that is **immune to error of both kinds**. We require a process that, on the one hand, does not stifle – and even encourages – creativity, but at the same time provides analytical validity. On the face of it, this is a contradiction,

53

since systematic analytical thinking is, to some extent, the antithesis of creativity, and vice versa. But I maintain that it is nevertheless possible to combine the two without detracting from either.

Proposal for an alternative Situation Estimate process

In approaching this task I utilized various models, mainly Prof. Philip Kotler's model of product development, as well as a brainstorming model derived from various sources. The theory that influenced me the most was Karl Popper's scientific methodology of "conjectures and refutations."

The process I propose consists of the following stages:

Stage 1: Learning the problem.
    A. Learning the parameters of the battlefield.
        1. The terrain.
        2. Relative combat power
        3. Space and time (and additional parameters).
    B. Learning the parameters of the mission.
        1. Learning the aim (as defined by the superior command level).
        2. Defining the mission (for myself).

Stage 2: Presenting possible courses of action (COAs).
    A. The unrestrained floating of ideas, according to the following principles:
        1. Deferring judgment: no COA is rejected in advance.
        2. Raising unconventional and "radical" COAs (thinking outside the box).
        3. Quantity: proposing as many COAs as possible (quantity leads to quality).

Stage 3: The commander selects the chosen course of action (CCOA)

    A. Rejection – examining the COAs in light of the Principles of War and the Warfighting Doctrine, and rejecting those that do not adequately meet these standards.

    B. Decision – choosing among the remaining COAs employing intuition.

These three stages engage the right hemisphere of the brain in the following way:

Stage 1 makes use of holistic perception. This is the stage at which the commander learns the parameters of the problem. Importantly, due to time limitations, he does not learn all the parameters, but only those most pertinent to the mission. His screening of the information is partly unconscious – that is where holistic perception comes in.

Stage 2 encourages creative and imaginative thinking.

Stage 3 makes use of analytical thinking, and later intuition.

The left hemisphere is utilized only in stage 3 - to eliminate unfeasible courses of action. The assumption that this is the correct use of analytical thinking is supported by two arguments. The first is derived from Popper's scientific methodology. Popper stresses that only refutation – as opposed to validation – is logically sound. The second argument arises from my empirical experiment (see the Appendix). While conducting this experiment, I initially attempted to assess the quality of courses of action by eliciting judgments, specifically of Command and Staff College instructors. However, I soon discovered that the reliability (i.e., consistency) of the judges was low when it came to giving positive judgments. That is, they rarely agreed on which was the best course of action.

Conversely, they did tend to agree on which options were bad. This strengthened my belief that analytical assessment is better suited to rejecting poor possibilities than to validating good ones.

Crucially, I believe that the quality of the CCOA (the course of action ultimately selected) depends on what happens at two key points in this process. The first is the stage of suggesting courses of action: it is crucial to suggest as many as possible. As researcher Dr. Dan Zakai says: "It is crucial to invest special efforts in considering alternative courses of action, using creative thinking and freeing oneself of past habits and mental preconceptions. Remember that one can never arrive at a plan that is better than the best plan considered." The second key juncture comes immediately after the elimination stage. At this stage, we should strive to be left with more than one good plan. As for the question of selecting among the remaining options – which are all good – I could suggest that the choice is random. Instead, I assert that the commander chooses among them in the manner I described in my discussion of dilemmas: using his supra-mental understanding and supra-sensory perception. But he must take care not to fall into a routine that renders his thinking predictable.

The process proposed here has an advantage over the standard one in that it prevents errors of omission by drastically widening the range of COAs considered. The following diagram exemplifies this:

Diagram 1 – Quality of COAs

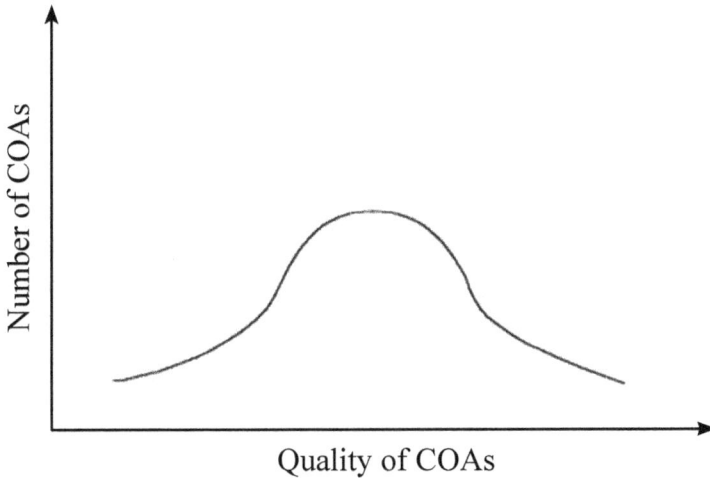

Quality of COAs

This diagram represents the "normal" distribution of COAs, where 100 represents a COA of average quality, and the standard deviation is assumed to be 15. The standard Situation Estimate process, which utilizes analytical thinking, produces **only** COAs in the middle range, the range between 80 and 120. It precludes COAs of sub-standard quality (below 80), but also COAs of excellent quality (above 120), which can only be produced through associative thinking.

The process I propose has the advantage of producing more COAs, of every quality, including both inferior *and* excellent ones. This advantage comes at a considerable risk: the risk of choosing a sub-standard CCOA. However, to guard against this problem – an error of commission – it includes sub-stage 3A (the stage of eliminating COAs), which is purely analytical, and involves organized and systematic thinking to avoid being tempted by fallacious ideas. In carrying out this stage, the guiding question should be: why is this COA not good? Only if this question cannot be answered does the COA make it to the next stage, at which the CCOA is selected.

I believe that through the use of this model – based on conjectures and refutations – we can beat any Turing machine.

On a routine visit to the brigade HQ in the Golan Heights, I passed by Mount Shifon. Hannan, a company commander in my battalion, sat beside me. Suddenly, he said, "The Shifon should be taken from this side." I looked at the mountain and then back at Hannan, and knew that he was right. I also knew he had not gone through all the steps of the Situation Estimate process. He had simply had a flash of inspiration.

Appendix

To determine the relative merit of the two Situation Estimate processes – the standard process taught to IDF officers and the one proposed by myself – I conducted the following experiment.

Introduction

Research objective – to determine which Situation Estimate process is better.
Secondary objective – to determine the quality of each process independently.

Criteria of analysis

I encountered some difficulty in formulating the criteria for judging the quality of the processes. Eventually I chose four criteria:

1. **Number of possible courses of action (COAs):** the larger the number of COAs proposed by the subjects, the better the process. This criterion was given a relatively large weight in the study, since there is a consensus among researchers

regarding its importance (Janis and Mann 1980, Zakai 1984, Caspi 1978). They agree that "one can never arrive at a plan that is better than the best plan considered" (Zakai 1984, p. 11).

2. **Number of different chosen courses of action (CCOAs):** The larger and more varied the set of CCOAs chosen by the subjects for the same problem, the better the process. This criterion is based on the assumption that a process yielding a wide range of CCOAs is more likely to achieve the element of surprise.

3. **Percentage of CCOAs derived from the first COA considered by the subject:** Researchers of decision-making processes often warn that, after a decision maker finds one option he likes, he will spend his time validating it and developing different versions of it, instead of considering alternative options (Janis and Mann 1980, Ahronson 1979). A procedure that yields a large number of CCOAs derived from the same initial COA is therefore an inferior one.

4. **Quality of CCOAs:** This was the most problematic criterion, because the reliability of the judges was low, making their opinions difficult to weigh. It was found that judges were relatively reliable in their negative assessment of CCOAs (this is consistent with Popper's observation that theories can be logically disproven but not proven). Hence, the criterion chosen was the number of CCOAs judged to be bad.

Method

Subjects:

The research subjects were 40 Command and Staff College students, divided into two groups of 20. The two groups were existing classes whose makeup was not determined by myself (I had no part in assigning students to the classes). Group A was subjected to tests 1 and 2, and Group B was subjected to tests 3, 4 and 5.

Tools

Operation order issued by commanding officer; map. Subjects were asked to choose a CCOA and plot it on the map.

Procedure

As part of the experiment, the subjects underwent two manipulations. First, they took a course to enhance their professional knowledge of the Principles and War and Warfighting Doctrine, and especially of the standard Situation Estimate process employed in the army. Then, they learned the alternative Situation Estimate process, and used it to select a CCOA.

No. of test	Date	Group	Situation Estimate process used	Before/ after taking the course
1	December 2, 1991	A	Standard	before
2	December 2, 1991	A	New	before
3	November 25, 1991	B	Standard	before
4	March 17, 1992	B	Standard	after
5	March 17, 1992	B	New	after

I tested the relative effectiveness of the two processes twice: one time before the students took the course (tests 1 and 2) and one time after they completed it (tests 4 and 5). I also checked how practicing the standard Situation Estimate process as part of the course affected the students› military thinking (tests 3 and 4).

Results

Following are the results of the experiment:

No. of test	Group	No. of subjects	No. of different CCOAs produced by the group	Average number of COAs proposed by each subject	Percentage of CCOAs derived from initial COA	No. of bad CCOAs
1	A	19	5	1.95	73%	0
2	A	19	8	3.53	26%	2
3	B	20	7	1.65	80%	2
4	B	17	2	1.53	76%	0
5	B	17	6	3.65	24%	0

Discussion

A. Number of COAs: In terms of this criterion, the results clearly indicate that the Situation Estimate process I propose is superior to the standard process. This is demonstrated statistically by a dependent samples t-test, which yields the following results (the data for group A is a comparison of tests 1 and 2; the data for group B is a comparison of tests 4 and 5):

Group	Prob [T] t-test	T	Std. dev	Mean	No. of subjects
A	0.0001	5.8834841	1.1697653	1.5789474	19
B	0.0001	8.2862689	1.0537049	2.1176471	17

B. Number of CCOAs derived from initial COA: this criterion also yields a decisive result favoring the process I propose. A dependent samples t-test confirms this (the data for group A is a comparison of tests 1 and 2; the data for group B is a comparison of tests 4 and 5):

Group	Prob [T] t-test	T	Std. dev	Mean	No. of subjects
A	0.0150	2.6887745	0.5972647	0.3684211	19
B	0.0035	3.3274528	0.6048053	0.4500000	17

C. Number of different CCOAs proposed by the group: The results for this parameter do not lend themselves to statistical analysis, but they too point in a definite direction. From a comparison of tests 3, 4 and 5, the following picture emerges: Before taking the course, the Group B students produced seven different CCOAs using the standard process. After taking the course, they produced only two CCOAs using the same process. Moreover, one of these CCOAs (attacking from the south) was proposed by 16 of the 17 students, whereas the second (attacking from the north) was proposed only by one. In other words, with the exception of one student, all the participants arrived at the same CCOAs (though there were two slightly different variations of this proposal). After learning the alternative Situation Estimate process (test 5), the group again yielded a larger number of different CCOAs (six different proposals).

The conclusion, I believe, is clear: during the course the students were «programmed» to produce similar output. However, the instructors at the Command and Staff College had a different opinion. When I presented them with my results, they asked,

«Was the course of action chosen by the students a good one?» When I replied that it was, they said, «Splendid. The plan was good and all the students arrived at it.» My answer to them is simple: «A predictable plan – no matter how good – is likely to fail, and therefore it is a bad plan.» I believe that criterion C, too, indicates the superiority of my procedure over the standard one.

D. Quality of CCOAs (i.e., number of bad CCOAs): this criterion, like the previous one, does not lend itself to statistical analysis. The picture it yields is less clear, but nevertheless interesting. The contrast between tests 1 and 2 exemplifies the risk associated with creative thinking, a risk mentioned by Eilam 1990, who says: «In procedural thinking, the risk of an error at some point of the process is accepted as an integral part of the method. In logical thinking, error is not possible as part of the method but only as a deviation from it.» (p. 9) Both these tests were conducted before the students took the course. In Test 1, using the standard process, no student chose a bad CCOA, whereas in test 2, using my process, two students selected a bad CCOA. However, in tests 4 and 5, conducted after the completion of the course, the students again employed my method, and this time the number of bad CCOAs was zero. From this I infer that the decisive factor was the knowledge of the Principles of War which the students acquired during the course. A good knowledge of these principles helps to prevent bad decisions. Hence, if my procedure is carried out by commanders with a good grounding in the Principles of War, and the last stage of my process is carried out accurately, so that each decision receives an analytical stamp of approval, errors of commission are avoided and the risk of which Eilam speaks remains hypothetical.

Problems with the study

The study suffers from two problems, both related to the sample of subjects. First, the sample (40 students) was insufficiently large; second, the assignment of subjects to groups was not random, since the groups were pre-existing college classes. Another disadvantage lies in the fact that the experiment was not conducted under laboratory conditions, but was a field study. As for the size of the sample, I believe the results of the study merit expanding it and applying it to additional populations.

Conclusion

In the classroom

The research hypothesis was that the Situation Estimate process proposed here is superior to the standard process used in the IDF. This hypothesis was confirmed by several criteria, namely the number of CCOAs produced by the group, the average number of COAs per subject, and the percentage of CCOAs derived from the initial COA. According to these criteria, the standard IDF procedure is ineffective: it does not produce a sufficient number of alternative proposals, and is therefore unsuited to dealing with the military problem, since it does not supply the element of surprise. The process proposed here is better in that it yields more alternatives, including creative ones, and therefore does supply this important element.

The fourth criterion – number of bad CCOAs – points to a possible disadvantage of the process proposed here. The risk, which stems from the possibility of committing errors of commission, is inherent in any creative process. However, the correct application of the analytical stage of my procedure effectively minimizes this risk.

The procedure also has a problem of external validity, stemming from the size and the character of the sample, and therefore I recommend to expand it and apply it to additional populations. If the results are replicated, I recommend replacing the standard process used in the IDF with the process suggested here.

On the battlefield

"Is the IDF capable of achieving surprise on the tactical level?"
"No!"
The analysis of test 4 demonstrated this, and also revealed the reason: over half of the students considered only one single alternative, and spent their time convincing themselves that it was right.

Conclusions:

1. **There never is, and never should be, a single plan that is considered best; this is an inherent characteristic of the military problem.**
2. **"Horizontal" thinking skills – imagination, creativity, intuition and holistic perception – are crucial to achieving victory on the battlefield.**
3. **The Situation Estimate process proposed here allows and encourages the employment of these skills, providing a relevant framework of application for each of them.**
4. **The stage of eliminating COAs lends the process the necessary analytical strength to guard against possible errors of commission.**

"MONETARY" LEADERSHIP

> *And the object of desire and the object of thought*
> *move in this way; they move without being moved.*
> *The primary objects of desire and of thought are*
> *the same.*
>
> (Aristotle, Metaphysics, Book XII, Part 7)

Military leadership is the power to mobilize people towards a goal. The theory of leadership, I propose in this chapter, combines variables that are often perceived as contradictory – and therein lies its advantage. It can explain a wider range of situations. (At the same time, it does not resort to truisms and tautologies, and as such it can be said to be empirical).

Analogy 1

When Sigmund Freud first published his theory of psychoanalysis, philosophers of science immediately attacked it on the grounds that it was not a science. Popper elucidated this objection by saying that the theory of psychoanalysis is not falsifiable: It is able to explain anything that happens in the field to which it refers, and therefore nothing is regarded as an observation that falsifies the theory. In other words, it can explain everything, and therefore can explain nothing (Popper K. *Conjectures and Refutations The Growth of Scientific Knowledge*. London: Routledge and Keegan Paul, 1963, pp. 34-35). However, given that psychoanalysis has helped many people lead a more contented life, and given that it achieved this regardless of whether or not it is a science, I believe that the broad explanatory power of psychoanalysis has its advantages.

Analogy 2

In the years-long struggle between the "engineering approach" to economy (centralized preplanning) and the "economic approach" (market forces), the fall of the USSR in the 1990s ruled in favor of the latter. The model of leadership proposed here is based on the claim that, in a military unit, there are forces at play that resemble the forces of the market, and which the commander must harness in steering and directing his unit. A common mistake, however, is to think that he can influence the very existence of these forces.

Analogy 3

The Scientific Management theory led to the development of the assembly-line method (which gained admiration that resembles our enchantment with computers). Several decades later, with the return to a human-centered approach to management, there was also a return to the combined method of labor, in which one worker performs a variety of tasks. Enrichment of the worker's experience is the main hallmark of this human-centered approach. The lesson to be drawn from this is that when we emphasize some goal or achievement at the expense of the human dimension, we may achieve momentary progress, but this progress will always be followed by regression.

The nature of military leadership

Military leadership differs from most types of leadership in the modern Western world (e.g., political or economic leadership). The difference between them – which goes to the very essence of military leadership – is that other types of leadership involve taking people where they *want* to go. The famous American businessman Lee Iacocca stated it well. He said: "Talk to people in their own language. If you do it well, they'll say, 'God, he said exactly what I was thinking.' And when they begin to respect you, they'll follow you to the death. The reason they're following you is not because you're providing some mysterious leadership. It's because you're following them." Endorsing this kind of approach, Shlomo Lahat (known by his nickname "Chich"), who was mayor of Tel Aviv for many years, ran the city according to opinion polls he conducted. He would find out what the people wanted and then carry out their wishes, as far as he could. I am not saying this to criticize him; on the contrary, this is the essence of democracy. The municipality and its various institutions exist to serve the people (i.e., meet their needs in the domains of culture, security, etc.), and therefore the leaders of a city must respond to the public's demands.

This is not the case for military leaders. An army commander must lead his troops towards goals and targets that are dictated from above, targets that neither he nor his troops chose. Moreover, he must lead them to places where they may meet injury or even death.

The meaning of the contradictions

It was very difficult for me to understand and accept the contradiction. The difficulty stemmed from my being a member of Western civilization, which is founded upon mathematical and logical thinking, at the basis of which lies the Law of Contradiction, which states that nothing can be simultaneously true and false.

An incident that occurred in my battalion got me thinking about the nature of courage and fear, which until then I had thought I understood. It was the incident of the command car that turned over, which I mentioned in the first chapter. The one responsible for the accident was a deputy company commander. On the face of it, the matter was simple: accidents happen, and the only required response was to punish the deputy commander and then go back to business as usual. However, when it happened a warning light came on in my mind. This deputy commander had been involved in three accidents within a six month period, one of them deadly. (The latter accident occurred before the deputy joined my battalion; the other two, less serious, occurred after he joined it).

After questioning the deputy and conducting other investigations, I asked my superior, Brigade Commander Ravve, to dismiss the deputy. Ravve was somewhat taken aback, because he knew me well, and knew that in the 22 months I had served as battalion commander I had not dismissed a single officer, though God knows I had officers who were less competent than the deputy. Ravve therefore asked me to sleep on it and to give him my final answer in the next day. When I came back in the morning with the same answer, he asked, "Why?" I answered, "Because he is not afraid. His fear threshold is too high, and as a result he fails to learn from his mistakes. This means that the next accident is only a matter of time."

Ravve approved the dismissal, and I thanked him for the extra night he had given me to think, because it was during that night that I realized that fear was a necessary component of courage. Without fear there can be no courage. Fear is awareness of danger, and courage enables us to face the danger. I do not just mean that courage is the means to overcome fear, but that courage is found only in those who feel fear. The two go hand in hand. After that night I understood her words: "Discard the dichotomous logic of zero and one in domains where they have no relevance."

Staff meeting ahead of a five-week training period:

Present are company commanders Ofer and Hannan, and operations officer, Sharon. I begin by saying: "We have five weeks of training ahead of us. Sharon has the list of allocated resources. I want you to consider what you want to achieve during the training, determine your priorities, and draft your plans accordingly. Tomorrow I'll approve them." Ofer asks for more details, and I say, "How about a cup of coffee?" While Dalia prepares our coffee, he repeats, "You haven't given us enough details." Before I can answer him the door opens and in comes the major general, who says, "Let's have those details." Immediately after him comes the chief-of-staff, who says, "No, delegate authority, let your men take the initiative."

The Major General: "Give them discipline!"

The Chief-of-Staff: "Encourage *esprit de corps*!"

The Major General: "Build up their professionalism!"

The Chief-of-Staff: "Build up their independence!"

Having delivered their piece, the major-general and the chief-of-staff turn on their heels and vanish from the room as if they had never been there. I am left confused. I looked at Ofer, Hannan, and Sharon and wonder what it is about these boys that makes me love them.

After some confusion I understood the source of the apparently conflicting advice of the major general and the chief-of-staff. A glance through the book *On Leadership,* published by the Ministry of Defense, told me that they represented different schools of leadership. The chief-of-staff represented the tradition of the Palmach[8] and the Paratroopers, whereas the major general represented the tradition of the British army and the Armored Corps. I thought all I had to do was figure out which school was more suitable for my battalion and its missions, or more suitable for the battlefield, and choose that school. But this was an illusion. A closer investigation reveals that overemphasis on discipline leads to disaster, and overemphasis on independently-thinking commanders leads to catastrophes no less horrible – and proof of this is all around us.

In a meeting with the developers of the Merkava 3 tank, held at the brigade before we incorporated the tank into our forces, I learned a lesson about discipline. I arrived at the meeting after a night in the field – one of Company Commander Shahar's exercises – and I was bone tired. I sat there, half dozing and

---

8   Palmach: the military arm of the Haganah, which served as the army of the Jewish Yishuv during the British Mandate. The Palmach created a unique climate of fighting, pioneering and command. Due to shortage of means, its members excelled at improvising, initiative and independent action. They had a great impact on the State of Israel and its army.

half listening. Through my dreams, some of which were daydreams, I heard the head of the tank development authority tell a story about an American tank crew that had fired faulty ammunition. They used the faulty ammunition it because they were afraid to report it, and this that was because every report of this kind meant a court martial, and every court martial meant punishment. So they preferred to fire it anyway, and as a result the tank commander and gunner were killed. The story managed to penetrate my consciousness and gave me an insight. I realized that discipline should never be sanctified above other values.

Reading on in the book *On Leadership*, I encountered the story of Dani Mass and the Convoy of Thirty-Five. It was a story I had never understood, and this time I found it even harder to understand. The story was presented as a shining model of independent commandership, but the more I thought about it the more it seemed like a huge fiasco. After all, the convoy was an abysmal failure. Platoon Commander Dani Mass made a bad decision that led to the death of 35 soldiers – elite troops – and failed to accomplish his mission.[9] The lesson I drew from

9   The Convoy of Thirty-Five was a platoon of fighters who set out on foot to resupply and reinforce the besieged kibbutzim of Gush Etzion during Israel's War of Independence, but were spotted and killed on the way. In the IDF heritage, their story has become emblematic of two supreme values: dedication to the mission and independent decision-making. During the mission, Dani Mass, the platoon commander, was faced twice with the decision whether to abort or postpone the mission, or to carry on, and on both occasions he chose to continue. The first occasion was at the start of the mission. The convoy was scheduled to set out at 19:00, but the preparations took longer than expected and the convoy was ready only at 23:00, giving the fighters less time to reach their destination before sunrise. Mass decided to set out anyway. The second occasion came during the march itself, when the convoy was spotted, apparently by an old shepherd which the

this story was that the value, or principle, of dedication to the mission must not be sanctified above other values either.

Gradually, the picture became clear. Additional examples in which values were taken to the point of *reductio ad absurdum* made me realize a basic truth: That none of the values of leadership idealized by the IDF are absolute, i.e., can always be regarded as the value from which all practical conclusions can be drawn. By analyzing additional examples I discovered that values like morale, *esprit de corps*, delegation of authority, "follow me," first into battle, etc., can sometimes lead to disaster or cause a catastrophe. Anyone who has ever commanded a unit knows that strict discipline, externally imposed, suppresses initiative and imagination and lowers morale. However, a unit with morale but without discipline will do even worse than a unit with discipline but without morale, and both will do worse than a unit that possesses a medium or high level of both. The conclusion is that a certain balance must be found between the soldiers' discipline on the one hand and initiative and independence on the other. This is a function with many variables that must be maximized. However, if the variables are sanctified and treated as absolute and immutable constants, it becomes impossible to reach optimum ("constrained optimization," in mathematical terms). I came to believe that a new understanding of leadership was needed, one based on these insights. However, here I encountered a difficult problem.

---

fighters apprehended but then released. Dani Mass again chose to continue the mission, despite the danger that the shepherd would alert the Arab villagers to the convoy›s presence. The convoy was indeed discovered and fought a courageous battle in which all of its fighters were killed.

I mention this story not to criticize Dani Mass, but to challenge the idea of sanctifying dedication to the mission over all other principles.

I was afraid to start rolling this heavy boulder before acquiring further tools.

The theory of effectiveness

The energy I needed to start rolling the boulder was provided to me by Benny, the brigade commander, who inspired me to come up with a "theory of effectiveness." The main principle of this theory is "do whatever most effectively serves the organization and its goals." Though seemingly self-evident, this directive actually demands a high level of awareness and self-discipline. The commander is required to do not what he instinctively wants to do, but what is likely to yield the best results. To better understand this theory, let us examine one of its applications: the art of giving feedback (which is a factor in motivating people). The goal of feedback is to improve the performance of the person receiving it, and this goal determines the content of the feedback. That is, the giver of feedback must say whatever achieves this goal most effectively, rather than what is strictly true – because in many cases bald truth will damage performance rather than enhance it. Feedback must first of all be designed to create receptiveness in the addressee, i.e., a willingness to accept further comments. Achieving receptiveness depends on the addressee's character: some will respond better to a caress and others to a slap in the face. It also depends on timing: some people will respond to a caress at one time and to a slap at another. If the feedback is aimed at more than one addressee, it is best to begin with a caress (i.e., positive feedback). In every exercise there are good points and bad, and if you begin with the good points, your audience will also be receptive to the bad ones. However, if you begin with the criticism, your audience will hear nothing and no progress will be made.

I mentioned that this method requires a high level of awareness and control on the part of the commander. This is because, in many instances, your gut screams for you to respond – "this blunder must not go unanswered, it requires a harsh response, etc." But the response must nevertheless be withheld if it is likely to produce a regression rather than progress. In such a case, you must not speak out, even if speaking out would make you feel better (on the level of results your good feeling counts for nothing).

The theory of effectiveness allowed me to reexamine the values of leadership from a new perspective. The insight it afforded was very significant. I understood that values – such as discipline and personal example, for instance – were ultimately means of motivating people, means of impelling them towards a goal, and must be presented as such. This perspective provides an effective way to deal with dilemmas. When faced with a situation in which two values conflict, choose the one that has the greater motivating power (at that particular point in time).

For instance, take the value of setting a personal example. A soldier (whether a plain common soldier or a commander) has no right to demand or even expect his superior officer to set a personal example. Rather, personal example is a tool that the commander possesses and which enables him to better motivate his men. Using Kant's terms, I might say that the absolute directive that lies at the basis of any military organization is to follow orders. But since I am exempt from employing overly-sharp analytical tools, and since the purpose of an order is to impel troops towards a goal, if there is a means that allows me to achieve this goal more effectively, I will always welcome it.

Leadership is the art of motivating people.
Motivation can be external or internal.
Internal motivation is more effective.

The components of leadership

Leadership has three components: The motivator, the motivated, and the motivation. A good combination of the three facilitates the effective movement of a unit (or an organization) towards its target.

The motivator (the commander)

If leadership is the art of motivating people, then the effectiveness of a leader depends on the range of manipulations he can perform. This range depends on certain characteristics and traits of the commander: high intelligence, for example, provides certain abilities, whereas developed sensitivity provides others; even the look of the commander's smile may grant him particular abilities of manipulation abilities. Charisma is the sum total of an individual's manipulative abilities. The more extensive these abilities, the more developed the individual's leadership skills, that is, the more varied the range of populations he can lead. (Hence the importance of self-awareness in a manager, for he must be aware of his abilities and know which of them to apply to a particular group with particular characteristics).

The motivated (the unit)

When we say that a particular kind of leader emerges in a particular culture, we mean that, in one culture, high intelligence might enable a leader to exercise ten different manipulations, for example, whereas in another culture it might enable him to exercise only five. Conversely, in the first culture strictness might provide him with only five manipulations, and in the second culture, with ten.

Example: every military unit has a personality of its own. This personality does not depend on the character of any one of its members, and it may remain more or less constant for years, just like an individual's personality. The nature of this collective personality can be discovered by isolating an "average member" of the unit and studying his character. This personality is composed of certain mental skills, emotional traits, etc., – and it determines what kind of personality the leader of the unit must have. In a certain unit, traits like strictness and centralized management may be more effective than high intelligence (though high intelligence in addition to strictness and centralized management will naturally produce even better results).

I discovered the importance of this correlation between the motivator (the leader) and the motivated (those he leads) through an error I made in appointing one of my company commanders. Ze'evi was an excellent commander for K Company, but when I transferred him to M Company he took a very long time to find his feet. The reason was that the range of manipulations he was capable of performing was highly effective with K Company, but not with M Company. I applied this lesson in the case of Rotem, when I considered appointing him company commander. Rotem's professional qualifications were very good, which, on paper, made him a fine candidate for the post. But in discussing the matter with Brigade Commander Ravve, I advised against choosing Rotem. When Ravve asked me why, I explained that my decision had nothing to do with

Rotem's qualifications. Rather, it had to do with the fit between him and myself: in my personal interactions with him, I had found him unpredictable and difficult to steer. I could not figure out what made him tick.

The fit between a commander and his subordinates is very important, but even when the fit is good, we often see difficulties and conflicts between the commander and his men. In such cases, the relevant tools of manipulation must be employed in order to solve the problems. Let me clarify with two examples. The first involves Tzahi, who was Eyal's deputy when Eyal was commander of L Company. Six months before the end of his term as commander, Eyal had to go abroad and Tzahi was required to fill his place. Tzahi's standing with the men was not good, and everybody – the company, Tzahi and myself – realized that the coming period would be tough. The question I asked myself was: How do I strengthen Tzahi's status and help him improve his leadership skills?

Considering this question, I remembered a story She had told me. In an experiment, a group of subjects were placed in a room and asked questions to stimulate a debate. At the same time, the participants were also subjected to a manipulation. The experimenters chose one individual whose skills were actually subpar, compared to the group, but whenever he spoke a green light came on over his head. The result was that his opinions gradually gained influence and his status in the group rose. I decided to conduct a similar experiment. I summoned the company staff to discuss the state of the battalion, the work schedule, and other matters. As far as I was concerned, the topic was of marginal importance; the important point was the manipulation. Whenever Tzahi spoke, I listened attentively and nodded in agreement at every full stop, and when he finished his remarks I said, "That's right." I repeated the experience experiment ten days later, to strengthen the effect.

Eventually, Eyal and Tzahi both finished their tours of duty and Shahar, who had been a platoon commander at the time of the experiment, became operations officer, and later, company commander. In that period, I had many conversations with him. One day I mentioned, as if offhandedly, the time when Eyal was abroad and Tzahi filled in for him. Shahar said, "I don't know exactly what happened, but that was the only time Tzahi functioned properly in the company." It is quite possible that other variables were also at play, but I believe that my manipulation was largely responsible for Shahar's impression.

Another tool I employed was the Pygmalion effect (the self-fulfilling prophecy). I used it with several people, but I shall describe only the case of Izhar, which illustrates the effect most clearly. When Izhar was appointed platoon commander in the company, he had several altercations with Ofer, the company commander. There was some tension between them that I found difficult to explain, but which clearly stemmed from peripheral matters that had nothing to do with Izhar's performance. To improve the situation, I made sure to remind Ofer every once in a while of Izhar's excellent abilities and to praise him for his performance of various tasks. I did this three or four times. One day, when I visited the battalion after finishing my course of duty, Ofer told me that Izhar was the best platoon commander he had ever had. When I heard this I smiled to myself, thinking, "It worked!"

We see, then, that circumstances are not always ideal. It is not always possible to find the right commander for a particular unit or the right unit for a particular commander, regardless of whether the commander or the unit are good in themselves. The problem is not merely finding a match. As superior officer, you must maximize the fit between the unit and the commander. This may require you to shave off a corner here or glue on a corner there, and this is done by means of motivational tools. A high awareness of the possible pitfalls, and of the tools and their proper use, can help solve many problems and smooth the way forward.

Motivation

If no single principle or value can always provide the solution, or form an Archimedean point from which to leverage the entire military system, the conclusion is that we must think in terms of reaching equilibrium. As part of this approach, we assume that within any unit, there are forces at play that resemble the forces of the market; moreover, there are ways to trigger or direct these forces. However, it is completely impossible to determine, define or control them absolutely (and hence there is always a measure of uncertainty in the results we obtain).

As an analogy consider the market itself. Generally speaking, there are always people who want to invest, but the extent of their willingness to invest depends on the interest rates. Economic leaders know that reducing the interest rate encourages investments, while increasing it discourages investments. The situation in a military unit is similar. Consider the forces of morale and initiative. They are determined mainly by two other forces, namely discipline and centralized control (i.e., the restricting of authority to the higher ranks). The correlation between the forces is shown in the following diagram:

Diagram 2

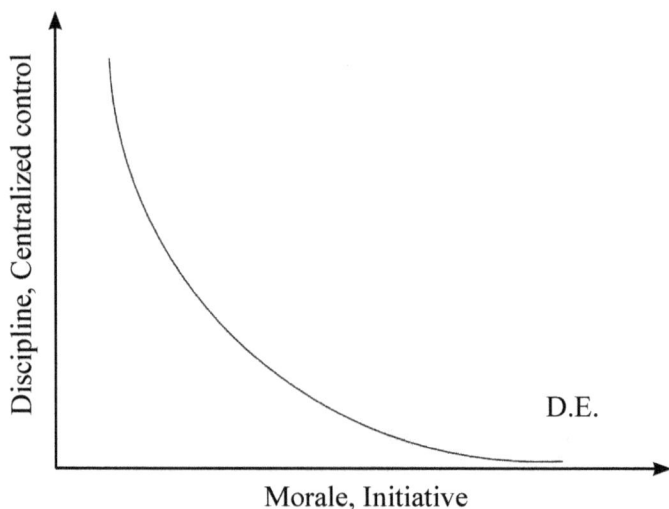

D.E.

Morale, Initiative

(y-axis: Discipline, Centralized control)

To put it verbally, when a commander increases discipline and centralized control within his unit, morale and initiative decline, and vice versa.

The importance of this model is that it defines the tools and methods that can be used. In this case, the tools at the commander's disposal are discipline and centralized control, because those are the parameters he can manipulate. Initiative, on the other hand, is beyond his direct control. Can a commander order his subordinates to show initiative? Ridiculous as it sounds, I have seen commanders try to do this. The reason, I think, is that they were raised on the engineering approach.

The curve in Diagram 2 consists of "efficient points," as they are termed in economy: possible points of equilibrium between the two forces we mentioned (discipline/centralized control and morale/initiative). A unit may deviate from this curve, but only for a short period of time. Since the curve consists of "efficient points," the unit will always tend to return to it. Hence, it is unwise to try and achieve a high degree of both discipline/centralized control and morale/initiative. If this can be achieved at all, it can only be achieved temporarily, and at the price of exhausting the unit. The problems that exist in most military units do not arise because these units are on some point on this curve (this is inevitable, as I mentioned). Rather, they stem from the fact that the unit is on the *wrong* point of the curve.

Precisely where a unit should be on this curve depends on where this curve intersects with the curve of military tasks. The task curve describes the precise ratio of initiative and discipline needed to handle a specific military task in the best possible manner. Military tasks fall into two categories, depending on the number of sub-battles that can be lost. The first category comprises tasks where no sub-battle may be lost. A radical example of this kind of task is operational activity on the border. The second category comprises tasks where each sub-battle is of minor importance compared to the overall picture. A typical example of this kind of task is handling the Intifada.[10]

---

10 "Intifada" (Arabic "shaking off," "rebellion," "uprising") was the name given to the Arab popular uprising in Gaza and the West Bank. The first intifada broke out in late 1987 and ended in 1994 with the signing of the Oslo Accords. This book speaks of the first year of the uprising, when the IDF had to deal, for the first time, with continued attacks on its forces by crowds armed with stones and clubs.

And since the tasks fall into two categories, so do the solutions. From the perspective of the forces in the field, operational activity on the border requires technical solutions. Each problem has a suitable solution that must be carried out "by the book," as far as possible. Conversely, handling the Intifada requires tactical (and even creative) solutions. Hence, in border activity – and in most defensive missions – the parameter of discipline is highly important. Conversely, in managing the Intifada, initiative and independent thinking are more important, as shown in Diagram 3.

Diagram 3

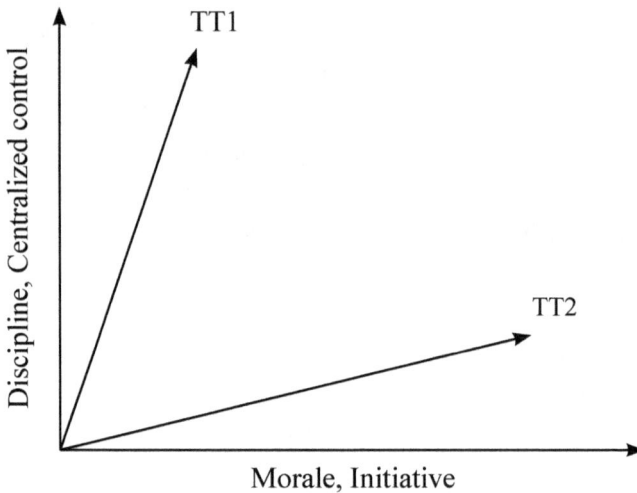

The precise angle of the line that represents the desired discipline/initiative ratio is determined by the character of the task.

TT1 – The desired ratio in preventing border infiltrations
TT2 – The desired ratio in handling the Intifada

A commander must ensure that his unit is always at the point of intersection between the discipline/initiative curve and the task curve (point E in Diagram 4), namely the point of equilibrium representing the precise ratio of discipline and initiative needed for the task at hand.

Diagram 4

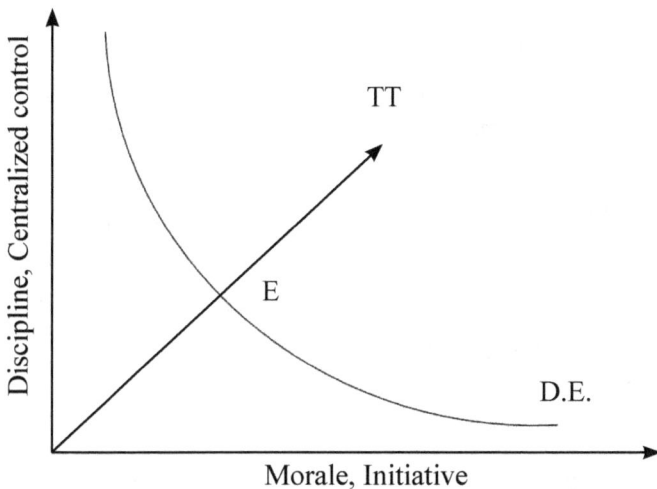

Now, let me explain how this model is realized (first a verbal explanation and then a graphic one). On the border, the commander must relieve the staff and secondary units of authority and take the decisions upon himself, while increasing the level of discipline. I discovered the truth of this while investigating an accident that occurred in the battalion that replaced mine on the Lebanon border. The accident was caused by lack of discipline and centralized control, and resulted in the death of a tank driver. Conversely, in activity in the West Bank, good results depend on encouraging initiative, independent thinking and (relative) freedom of decision among one's subordinates. The way to do this is to relax authority and discipline to some extent and delegate authority, thereby enabling initiative to emerge (Once it emerges, it can be further enhanced by additional means of motivation, such as various kinds of positive reinforcement).

When realized in practice, this model impacts a commander's most banal and day-to-day decisions. For example, if a company commander on the Lebanon border sends a crew member on a mission at his own discretion, while disregarding the alert-level dictated by his superiors, the battalion commander must not overlook this. However, if a company commander does the same thing as part of operational activity in the West Bank, it might be warranted acceptable to overlook his violation.

The scenarios of which I am thinking as I write these lines are ones in which one force is relieved by another, whether on the Lebanon border or in the West Bank. On the Lebanon border, whenever a new force came to replace my own, I constantly stayed on the radio, receiving status reports, giving orders and supplying solutions, and I personally led one of the relief convoys. Conversely, in the West Bank, I would take the replacing battalion commander on a tour of the area, and we would break contact with the staff. This created a dynamic in the battalion whereby people worked independently and it was felt that intervention on my part would only be disruptive.

Diagram 5

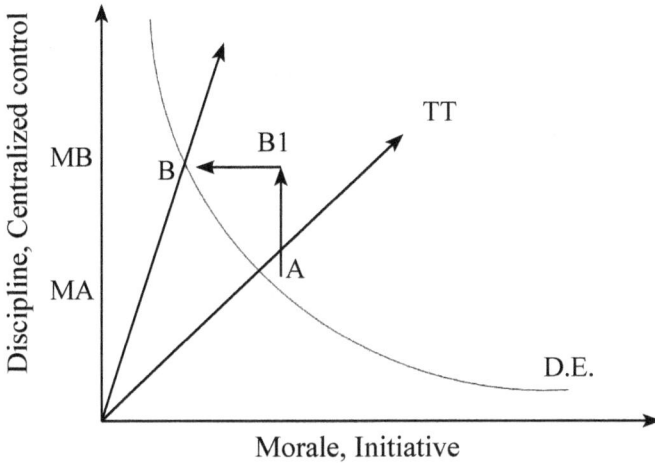

Morale, Initiative

Transitioning from one type of activity to another requires shifting form from one point on the curve to another. Consider a battalion engaged in training, a task represented by line TT1 in Diagram 5. The battalion's discipline/initiative ratio is at a particular point of equilibrium, represented in the diagram as point A. If the battalion is transferred to the Lebanon border, for example, the TT line moves left, to TT2. If the commander leaves the level of discipline unchanged, at point MA, then the battalion will not be in equilibrium, and the result will be multiple mishaps. To reestablish equilibrium, the commander must raise the level of discipline from point MA to point MB. At this juncture the battalion's discipline/initiative ratio will momentarily move to point B1. But then the internal forces within the battalion will cause it to slip back into equilibrium, at point B, where it can stay for a time. If the battalion is then transferred to the West Bank, the commander must affect a shift from point B to point C. This is done by delegating authority

Yotam Gadot

and relaxing discipline. At first, the battalion will shift to point C1 in Diagram 6. But subsequently internal forces will cause equilibrium to reestablish itself at point C.

Diagram 6

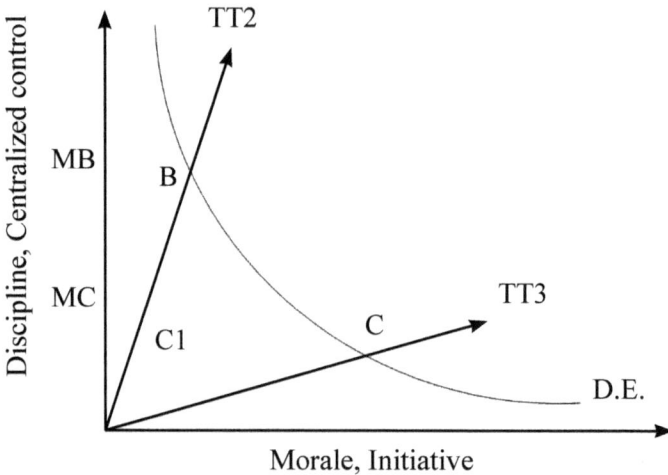

Morale, Initiative

Analysis of TT curve angles according to character of task (Diagram 7)

In Diagram 7, the leftmost curve (TT1) and the rightmost curve (TT2), represent activity on the Lebanon border and activity in the West Bank, respectively. The lines do not converge on the X and Y axes because some degree of discipline and initiative is always needed, if only a minimal degree. Defensive battles (TT3) will generally be in the region of TT1, because (as a rule) they require more discipline than initiative, whereas offensive battles (TT4) will be in the region of TT2, because

88

(as a rule) they require more initiative than discipline. The more technical the mission, the more important the factor of discipline and less important the factor of initiative. For example, an assault breaching mission (clearing a path through obstacles such as mines) is an offensive-type mission, but it is mostly technical, and therefore it will be closer to TT3 than to TT4 on the graph.

Diagram 7

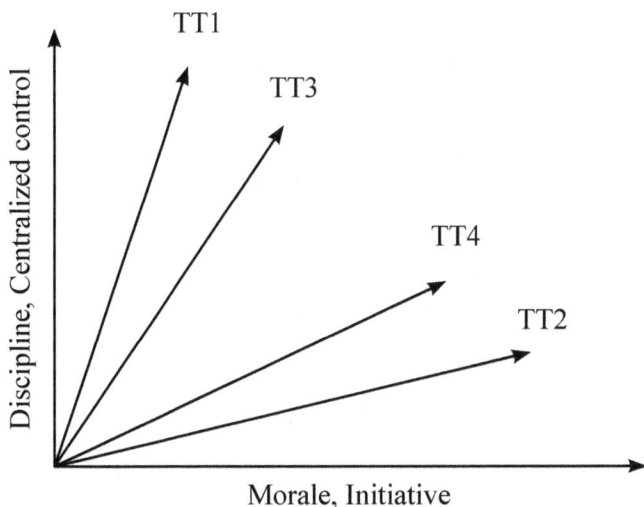

Definitions

Indirect motivating force:

A force that always exists in the unit, and which the commander cannot affect directly, but only indirectly – such as morale, initiative, cohesion. Harnessing this force will have an impact on any operation the unit performs, whether it is operating in Lebanon or defending a weapons depot in the Golan Heights.

Direct motivating force:

A force that always exists in the unit, but which the commander can affect directly – such as discipline, centralized control, delegation of authority, loyalty, and decision-making processes. These elements too have an impact on any operation the unit performs.

Motivational tools:

A force that exists in potential, and can be used only in the context of a specific mission or definite goal – such as the Pygmalion effect (self-fulfilling prophecy), setting a personal example, or addressing an individual's needs.

It is important for the commander to be familiar with these forces and motivational tools, and know not only how to use them but also what his limitations are (the limitations built into the system, not his own personal limitations). This may the place to voice several warnings about mistakes I made as a beginner and later saw others make as well:

1. **Chasing illusions:** A commander must not expect to achieve both a high level of discipline and a high level of initiative. I myself fell into this trap once, as a young platoon commander, when I imposed strict discipline and then wondered why my staff was not showing initiative. It took me a while to realize that they were afraid to overstep the line and incur punishment.

2. **The absolute constant of behavior:** I once knew a commander who used to tell his men: "Come to me with any problems, come into my office, don't be shy." But the door to his office was always closed. The closed door said:

"Don't come in, don't come to me with problems," and it spoke louder than the commander himself. Everything a commander does sets something in motion, and he must have the sensitivity to know what message he ultimately conveys (this, without even addressing the problem of what message the others receive).

3. **Logic plays little part in the theory of motivation:** I can present numerous examples to demonstrate that each motivational tool is more powerful than logic, but I will suffice with what I once wrote to a friend, to convince him that loyalty is more powerful than logic:

A commander who disobeys his superiors will not be obeyed by his subordinates. When they see him disobeying an order they will learn from his example. Subsequently, no matter how much he bolsters his orders with persuasive reasoning and arguments, they will do as they see fit… Being loyal to your commanders will make it easier to motivate your own troops.

The conclusion is that no matter how right you are, and no matter how smart you are, you must always remember the motivating forces at play. These forces never sleep, even when you do (and incidentally, your sleep – how much you sleep and when – also sends a message and affects motivation), so you must use them wisely to direct your men.

1. **In every unit, direct and indirect motivating forces are constantly at play.**
2. **Every commander has potential motivational tools at his disposal, which can be employed in a specific mission or to achieve a particular goal.**
3. **The commander must motivate his men through correct use of the motivating forces and motivational tools.**

Addendum

The importance of mistakes: Now that I am exempt from the
Law of Contradiction, I find it easier to discuss the importance –
the supreme importance, in my opinion – of mistakes. The
story begins with a casual remark She made when She told me
about the first patient She treated. "It was the mistakes I made
in this treatment," She said, "that caused it to be effective."
This remark took me far away from our little kitchen and the
two cups of coffee, to that rocky field north of the Lebanon
safety security zone and the incident of Hamtzani's leg. When
I saw Hamtzani's leg fly off, I thought, "shit!" But later that
same night, in the hospital, I understood that something good
had happened to me. I was free of my obsession. From the
moment I crossed the border and set foot in Lebanon, I had
been gripped by the fear of making a mistake. But now that
I had made it, I felt free. Now, I thought, I would be able to
focus on what needs to be done, and not on the horrible thing
that might happen. Now I too am burdened with the weight of
error, a weight that can sometimes be sweet.

What I mean to say is that a commander's mistakes can
sometimes release something within him: energies of
leadership that otherwise he wouldn't have been able to tap.
Taking this one step further, we might say that some mistakes
have to be made, because without making them one cannot be
a good commander.

An impossible situation is one in which a commander
or unit are is given a mission that is impossible for them to
accomplish. Example: a tank commander fresh out of the
course joins a battalion tasked with defending the border.
If you place him with a veteran crew – for instance in an

outpost that has only one tank crew – you place him in an impossible position. The dynamic may play out as follows: At 2:00 in the morning, in the middle of an ambush, one of the crew members will suggest listening to the radio (to avoid falling asleep). The tank commander will try to object, saying that this is against regulations, but the crew members will reply that this is their fourth time on the line and they have always listened to the radio. I can continue fleshing out the scenario, but there is no need. Ultimately he will let them listen to the radio, since they pose a greater threat to him than his superiors, namely the company commander or the battalion commander, who are not supposed to find out in the first place – unless something goes wrong.

But go wrong it will. And if, following the fiasco, I had to court martial this tank commander, I don't know what punishment I would give him. In any case I am sure I would find it difficult to look him in the eye. Any commander, regardless of seniority, professional ability and powers of motivation, can be placed in an impossible situation – but decency compels us to never cause this to happen to do so. This is perhaps the only important value to be conveyed in the teaching of leadership: never place your subordinates in situations they will find impossible.

CONVICTION, MORALITY AND MORALE

Where there is no bad,
and no good,
there lies hell.

"When Rabbi Ragesh led his people into the caves – and I did
not know then, Rabbi – and they followed, the people waited
to die. That's not the way. We've died for too long. It's their
turn now."
(Howard Fast, *My Glorious Brothers*)

During a simulation, I asked my staff to imagine the following
scenario:
Nighttime in the kasbah[11] of Salfit. The stone houses are silent.
Each stone, you realize, can be hurled at you tomorrow and
hit you or one of your comrades. It can hit the command car
windshield, causing the driver to lose control. It has been a
difficult day. A day of chasing after stone-throwers of varying
ages. In the morning, kindergarten kids, in the afternoon,

---

11 Kasbah: the ancient part of a Muslim town, usually an area of
    twisted, narrow alleys and sometimes also underground tunnels.

elementary school children, and in the evening, high school kids. The purpose of this nighttime raid is to surprise wanted terrorists in their homes. The mission is an important one: the terrorists of Salfit are notorious throughout the area.

The incident happens occurs in one of the homes. One of the soldiers identifies a teen who is lying in bed. The teen, realizing he had has been identified, jumps up, and starts to run away. After he is caught, one another of the soldiers continues to hit him. His arm is broken and he is taken to the hospital. The company commander must now conduct an investigation in an attempt to discover who hit the boy.

A difficult situation. On the one hand, the deed was an immoral one by any standard. On the other, cohesion and unity are important in the army, and with good reason. In their absence, the soldiers' ability to survive as a unit and as individuals is compromised. "Let there be no hope for informers," a Jewish prayer says. So what if this sentiment was expressed in Anti-Semitic Europe and was directed at the regime? It is an inevitable example of the result example of sanctifying cohesion for the sake of survival.

Very difficult! Imagine yourselves as the company commander, I said to my men. You sit alone in your office, which bears no resemblance to the office you left behind in on the permanent base in the Golan, and think back on to the year that has passed. For a year you have been commanding the company – on the Lebanon border, in training and in the Intifada. It has been a year of much toil and frustration, and now, just when you thought you had accomplished something, this had to happen. You wracked your brain thinking up the many quite a few ideas, methods and ways, you have employed, in order to achieve the level of cohesion that has you have finally been achieved. Knowing that this cohesion strengthens the troops and is therefore a great asset in combat, you wonder whether to you should put pressure on the company and to force them to divulge the name of the culprit. The question haunts you and will not give you rest. The price of applying pressure will be a less effective company: Less ready for war and also less able to perform its job here in Salfit. You never thought something like this could happen in your company.

The renowned contemporary English writer and philosopher E. M. Forster, who greatly cherished his country's culture and heritage, once said: "If I had to choose between betraying my country and betraying my friend, I hope I should have the guts to betray my country." Whereas some other Englishman, no less educated and cultured, might have said: "If I had to choose between betraying my country and betraying my friend, I hope I should have the guts to betray my friend." (Yeshayahu Leibowitz, "Laws and Values," in: Ishai Menuchin (ed.), *On Democracy and Obedience*, 1990).

The men pondered the scenario. The atmosphere in the battalion clubhouse was relaxed, the comfortable chairs and curtained windows making it difficult to concentrate on the simulation. Yet the debate nevertheless became lively and opinions were divided. Some of the platoon and company commanders advocated applying pressure and discovering the identity of the soldier who had beaten the teen, while others opposed this. After everyone had their say, it would be my job to step up and rule on the proper course of action. That is, to firmly decide what should be done in this situation, and how. And I did not know what to say.

The difficulty I experienced that day was but a pale reflection of the difficulty we all experienced at the start of the Intifada. We did not know what was right and what was wrong. When we found ourselves facing a riot, nobody knew what the desired outcome was: What accomplishment would justify saying that the unit had done its duty successfully? What counted as a good outcome and what counted as a bad one? The inability to define the quality of a given action – this lack of standards – was responsible for the feeling of hell that permeated some parts of the army.

But gradually and steadily the army formed standards for handling the Intifada, thus providing its units with clearer goals – which greatly improved the feeling of the commanders and soldiers. At the same time, new problems emerged, especially in the active service units. The problems stemmed from the fact that the standards, the parameters of failure and success, were different than in any other arena. When operating on the border, the mission is clear and the meaning of success is obvious: the task is to prevent any terrorist unit from reaching the fence. If a cell is discovered, eliminating it counts as success; wounding its members or driving them off counts as a partial success; and having the unit reach the fence counts as failure. Generally speaking, defending the border requires thwarting 100% of the infiltration attempts, by any means.

Conversely, in the West Bank, in the Intifada, the situation was completely different. Faced with 200 rioters in a narrow alleyway, the task was to disperse them with minimum casualties (this was before the IDF drafted regulations that allowed opening fire on masked rioters). Suddenly you had to give your men different instructions: Do your utmost not to injure, not to kill. This was the opposite of everything they had learned since they joined the army. Moreover, you had to accomplish this while "ploughing with an ox and a donkey together." You had to hold all your men to this standard, even though one was a hard-core hawk and the other a peacenik. Things were especially difficult for units that alternated between action in the West Bank and elsewhere. You had to "turn on a switch" in your head when you entered the West Bank and then "switch it off" again when you left it.

One week later, we had a real incident in Salfit.

Nighttime in the kasbah of Salfit. The stone houses are silent. The foot patrol, under platoon commander Izhar, sets out and encounters stone-throwers already at the yellow house. Izhar's superior, Ofer, calls the company into action and initiates flanking maneuvers. Some of the soldiers are hit by stones, and as the incident draws out, I realize that things are getting dicey. I dispatch the command group to Salfit. On the way, Ofer asks permission to open fire with special (non-lethal) weapons. I deny his request. "Be with you in two seconds," I tell him.

Reaching the entrance to the kasbah, I radio Ofer and ask him to direct me to the site of the incident, but five large rocks that threaten to smash the jeep make it eminently clear that I have stepped right in the middle of it. We retrace our steps. I join Ofer and he describes the exact location of the rioters and of our troops. "We command the high ground," he says. "All we need to do is to throw two shock grenades and then attack." I order him to attack, but without shock grenades or any other weapon. Ofer tries to say something, but he knows me, and knows that this time I am firm in my decision. So attack he does. The soldiers, for whom this is the first night in Salfit, are not familiar with the maze of alleyways, and when they reach the roof where most of the rioters were concentrated they find nothing but a pile of rocks waiting to be thrown.

After we returned the forces to the outpost, we gathered at the gate and perform an initial review of the incident. Ofer said, "We failed" (and I knew he wanted to add "because of you," but refrained out of deference to me). I replied, "Eventually we will win."

As I returned with the command group to the battalion camp, I was deeply troubled. I asked myself, "Did I place them in an impossible situation?" The question took me back to that afternoon, to the talk I gave the battalion before starting operational activities. In preparing my talk I had perused the handbook on the rules of engagement. As I leafed through it, I thought to myself that it was a fine legal document. A law student handing it in as a seminar paper would have surely received a good grade. But how, I asked myself, does one possibly convey its content in a 30-minute briefing? How will the most junior tank driver in the platoon, whom I plan to send to patrol the kasbah of Salfit in one hour, know when it is permissible to open fire and when it is not? Time was not on my side, of course. I had to decide right away. And since I believed the worse error would be one of commission (that is, that a soldier would fire unnecessarily), I decided to impose the strictest possible constraint: no firing at all.

That evening, in the tent still stifling from the heat of the day, the feedback did not take long to arrive. The company commanders Shahar, Ofer, Ze'evi and Yigar protested, "You are sending us into battle with our hands tied behind our backs." I asked, "How about a cup of coffee?"

After they left, I remained alone, staring at the Israeli flag to my right, and asking myself: Did I place them in an impossible situation? My thoughts wandered, trying to find their way through the "garden of forking paths" known as the Intifada. This is a labyrinth of dilemmas, each leading into another, making it impossible to calculate the outcome of any decision and therefore difficult to plot a course of action.

Throughout my career as battalion commander, Ben Gurion's famous statement always echoed in my ears: "Let every Hebrew mother know that she has placed the fate of her sons in the hands of worthy commanders." And I knew that every Hebrew mother who had placed her son in my hands would find me worthy on one and only one condition: that I brought her son back alive. And I also knew that the order to hold fire was placing my soldiers – the sons of those Hebrew mothers – at risk.

The temptation was great. My heart – not my philosophical mind but my heart as a man of action – whispered to me, "If the scenario you fear more than anything is facing an Israeli mother and saying 'I am responsible for your son's death', then the solution is simple. All you need do is relax the constraints a bit, loosen the rules of engagement. After all, you will not have to face the mother of any Palestinian boy. "That's not fair," challenged my mind. To which my tempted heart replied, "True, but so what? What does fairness have to do with it? What good is it? Fairness is required only when it serves society. When it does not serve the interests of society, it is no longer important."

There is something about the night that causes it to sharpen the senses and intensify the emotions. For this reason, nights can be wonderful but also terrible. This night could be either. If I found a solution, it would be good and even wonderful, but if I failed it would be terrible and even abysmal. The story of that night begins with the words of Martin Levi van Creveld, an Israeli military historian who wrote: "The real problem lies in fighting the weak. If you are fighting the weak, then when you lose you lose, and when you win you also lose." Van Creveld added: "This insight is missing from books of strategy, which is what prompted me to write my book. The idea originates with Nietzsche, who wrote: 'Nothing is more frustrating than never-ending victory or repeated victory'." Van Creveld's words, as you probably realize, were written under the blinding neon lights of university lecture halls. They are based on the assumption that the one holding the gun is necessarily the stronger party. The words of my company commanders, my operations officer and my deputy battalion commander prove otherwise – but their words never reached van Creveld's ears. Had he heard them, he would have probably asked: "If so, what then is the source of the stone-throwers' power? Why are they not weak, and why are we not strong?"

The first answer that springs to mind has to do with morality. Perhaps their military strength stems from their moral strength? But a closer examination reveals the falsity of this. Their strength stems from the simple fact that the battle is fought with stones, that it is fought with "ninjas" (the spiked caltrops scattered in on the road) and with burning tires. Their power stems from the fact that they are the ones dictating the rules of the game! And what allows them to dictate the rules of the game is the high moral standards of the Israeli army. No army in the world, and certainly in the Middle East, would have shackled itself with rules of engagement that completely prohibit opening fire.

Obviously, it can be argued that our moral problem lies in ruling over another people, that the occupation itself weakens us, no matter how we conduct ourselves. However, I am not a philosopher; the question that concerns me is a thoroughly practical one. I observe two rivals, and find them to be of equal strength. I therefore wish to understand what is weakening the side that is supposed to be the stronger one, namely the side that is wielding the gun. Since I have spoken with many soldiers in the battalion, and know that most of them do not see our presence in the West Bank as inherently immoral (and the depth of their philosophical thinking is immaterial, since all individuals are required to make moral judgements regardless of their philosophical education), the question remains why the battalion is losing its power.

The catalyst for my insight was a report I saw on the Friday night news program. It featured the mother of an officer who had fallen in the Lebanon war. She told how, on his last weekend at home, her son had spoken about his army service. When he described his experiences in Lebanon, she said to him, for the first time in her life, "You must refuse to serve there!" The next Sunday he returned to his unit, and several days later he was killed. I remember my reaction when I saw her on the show. The minute she mentioned telling her son that he must refuse to serve, I said to her image on the screen, "He is going to die." He will die because he will lose conviction in what he is doing, and conviction is essential for performing well.

This woman's son was not facing "blurry values" but rather "a crisis of values." Based on the fact that he elected to become an officer, I assume that, from childhood, he was brought up to do his duty. Suddenly he was told to refuse to serve. This rendered him helpless and powerless. It paralyzed him – making him terribly vulnerable. This insight is corroborated by a study that was carried out in the U.S. army among pilots in the Vietnam war. The study found a correlation between the depth of a pilot's' conviction and his chances of falling in battle.

*

The smell of gunpowder always carries with it thoughts of death, thoughts which arise regardless of the actual level of danger. Every fighter has his way of dealing with these thoughts. I developed my own coping strategy during the 1982-1983 Lebanon war. Whenever I find myself in danger I think of Bialik's poem "After My Death," and the lines in it that say: "And alas! One more tune that man had / And now that tune is forever lost / Forever lost!" Oddly enough, I reverse the sentiment, and draw encouragement from the poem. I believe that I still have one more tune inside me, and therefore I shall survive. I know that this belief – that I have one more tune in me – is the reason I am still alive.

I understood that the key was conviction: the conviction that you are doing what you must do. The Palestinian insurgents had plenty of conviction, but my soldiers did not. I realized that if I wanted to win this battle, I would have to fight for my soldiers' sense of conviction. They had to believe they were doing what they had to do (even if it was not necessarily the right thing to do) and, moreover, that they had the ability to do it. The next morning I launched my assault. I gathered the company commanders and told them of my nightly vigil. Then I said, "A soldier who does not believe he is doing what he **has** to do is a weak soldier. Hence, whoever is not totally comfortable with his presence here in the West Bank should not serve here at all." I stressed that I was not referring to soldiers who held the political view that Israel should withdraw from the West Bank. This political view has no impact on a soldier's ability. I meant that those soldiers who objected to serving in the West Bank but had not found the inner strength to refuse.

Hence, before the next round of operational activity, I devoted a training exercise to the battle for conviction. We analyzed scenarios and laid down boundaries for acceptable behavior. The goal was to set out crystal-clear moral standards. After this preparation, two soldiers approached me and asked to meet with me. One of them was a tank commander who had joined the battalion to participate in the military operations for the operational activity, the other was the battalion doctor, who approached me on behalf of his medics. The tank commander was confused. Talking to him I saw a man in the grips of a profound moral crisis. He had been raised to cherish both patriotic values and humanistic ones, and could not decide which set of values should take precedence at that moment in time (I privately noted another factor that affected him significantly, namely his social status as an outsider in the battalion). My talk with him was short and went more or less as follows:

He: "There are some tasks I cannot perform."
Me: "Such as?"
"Beating up locals or raiding the homes of innocent people at night."
"Why do you think you will be asked to do that?"
"Because that is what we do."
"What makes you think so?" (The soldier had never served in the Intifada before)
"Stories I've read in the papers and heard from friends."

After I clarified that he would not be required to beat anyone up or raid the homes of innocent people, he changed tack. "I do not wish to take part in ruling over another people. I feel I have no moral right to do so," he said.

I did not want to argue with him. I preferred that people who lacked conviction in the mission would not participate in operations in the first place. But what emerged from my lips was a different answer. "The question of serving in the West Bank is not as the philosophers describe it," I said. "It is more similar to Sophie's choice. It has nothing to do with the question of obedience, which is the topic of so many studies these days. The problem is different. The problem is that, if you do not serve here, someone else will, someone whose actions you cannot control. Of course, you might argue that, if all the soldiers refused to serve, Israel would have no choice but to withdraw from the territories. But that is clearly a fallacy, since if the majority of Israelis wished to withdraw from the territories, the makeup of the government would be different. Your choice, then, is between serving here yourself and leaving the task to others – people who are not morally conflicted and will presumably act worse than you, from a moral standpoint. Even if the actions you perform here are less than perfectly moral, you will still be doing some good, on in the balance. However," I added after a moment of silence, "I do not wish to enter into moral debates. That is a point that concerns me less, because I have settled the matter for myself. I want you to think about what I said and decide what you believe. If you find yourself fully convinced that it is the right thing to do, come with us tomorrow. If not, I excuse you from the mission."

The next day, I saw him boarding the bus with the rest of the men.

Comment: My statements above, and those below, will touch upon the moral issues but will certainly not exhaust them. My arguments are partial and cannot form the basis for drawing any definite conclusions. I do not wish the moral dilemma to distract the reader from my main point, namely the impact of conviction on a soldier's mettle.

In my next meeting with Brigade Commander Ravve, after the usual opening (what is called the expressive part of the meeting), I suggested that we appoint a "legitimacy officer" (a sort of "politruk" or political commissar) for the brigade. I stressed the importance of managing the soldiers' conviction – a point on which we naturally agreed – and said that I needed an officer to help me with this task, just as I had one to help me draw up operative operation plans. I added that even Judah Maccabee, whose leadership abilities are beyond question, had a "legitimacy officer" to help him, Rabbi Ragesh.

The legitimacy officer is in charge of managing the soldiers' awareness. A major part of this is seeing to their sense of conviction: imbuing them with a solid conviction that they are doing what they have to do. The murkier the moral situation, the greater the importance of this role. The legitimacy officer must deal with phenomena like "fuzzy norms" and help the soldiers settle moral conflicts. The IDF used to have officers of this sort, but it canceled this role because it was confident of the rightness of its path and of the psychological fortitude of its soldiers. But the Intifada, even more than the first Lebanon war, revealed the uncertainty and the lack of fortitude.

After I finished delivering this little speech, which I had prepared in advance, Ravve smiled a smile that said, "I agree with you but it's not realistic" – thereby burying my idea.

Two questions remain unanswered. First, what did I say to my staff at the end of the simulation, and second, how did the battalion handle the strict orders not to shoot? When I stood up to conclude the simulation, I thought we were at an impasse with no way out. But as I walked towards the podium, I had another idea. It is possible to bypass the problem altogether with a "vertical flanking" maneuver, I thought, and in the army this is permissible and even desirable. So I said: "The situation as it was described here is unsolvable. And it is well that we realize this now, because the lesson we must take from this analysis is that we need to be **smart.** That is, **we need to prevent such incidents from occurring in the first place.**

As for the rules of engagement, I modified them slightly – relaxed them a bit – authorizing the company commanders, and only them, to open fire under certain conditions. Interestingly, after the first week, during which each of them opened fire once, not a single bullet – either metal or plastic – was fired during the entire operational activity.

A soldier's mettle depends on his sense of conviction. By "sense of conviction" I mean two things: the conviction that he is doing what he has to do, and the conviction that he is able to do it.

OBSERVATIONS AND DOUBTS

(From the Diary of a Battalion Commander)

September 28, 1988 – Succeeded Tesler as battalion commander

October 1988

On the quality of the unit:

1. The quality of a unit depends on a wide range of variables, which the commander can manipulate in various ways. A discipline level of 9 on a scale of 1 to 10 has results in certain effects, and a morale level of 8 has others. The commander must find the right balance; he must optimize this multi-variable equation and try to maintain the best possible situation outcome over time. Since the unit in question is a dynamic body, constantly changing, the commander must make periodic adjustments, increasing certain pressures while easing others.

2. The quality of a unit cannot be measured by simply studying the internal processes that occur within it

(though improving these processes can increase the unit's effectiveness). Nor can its quality be gauged by measuring its success rate in one specific mission (because, by exerting unusual pressure during this that mission, the commander can might achieve a good positive outcome on a one-time basis). To determine the quality of a unit, its performance must should be measured over time (i.e., over a series of missions).

3. As for the correlation between the quality of the commander and the quality of his unit: if the commander is incompetent, the unit's performance will be poor, but a well-performing unit requires more than just a good commander.

November 1988

On discipline:

Discipline is an important factor in the reach of a commander's control, for it enables him to control subordinates who are not under his direct observation. Discipline is the keystone of the military. It is the central cog that moves all the other cogs. However, an army does not function on discipline alone; the keystone requires other stones to support it.

There are three types of discipline: Self-discipline, external discipline, and internal discipline. Self-discipline is a personal trait of character. External discipline is imposed by the commander upon his subordinates. (For example, when a commander court-martials a soldier, he is employing external discipline). Internal discipline is internally motivated, but is distinct from self-motivation. In both cases, the individual holds himself to a certain level of performance. But in the case of self-discipline, he does so because he wants to, and in the case of internal discipline, he does so because others – his commander and/or his comrades – expect him to (In the former case the source of motivation is internal, and in the latter case, external).

A commander should rely mainly on internal discipline to motivate his troops. Were it possible, I would recommend using this type of discipline exclusively. Excessive use of external discipline leads to disaster, and insufficient use of it can lead to disorder that undermines the unit's effectiveness. However, if the unit's internal discipline is strong enough, it is possible to do away with external discipline altogether. Hence, stress must be placed on cultivating internal discipline. And since the main point about discipline is that it must be internal, it does not matter whether your subordinates call you Battalion Commander or call you by your first name. The important point is that they know who holds them accountable for every decision and every action. They must know that every action must have a reason, preferably a good one, and that there is a system of law and order.

I believe that when a commander reaches this point with his unit, he has attained the ideal state in terms of discipline. With this kind of discipline he can reach each and every soldier (as company commander Avishai likes to emphasize). Before taking action, each and every one of his soldiers, no matter where he is and when, will visualize the commander and ask himself, "What would the commander do?" and "What would he say of what I am doing?" Once this situation is reached, even a simple soldier at 2:00 a.m. will think twice before doing something silly, and the chances he will do something silly therefore drop considerably.

This is the way to create the correct climate of command in terms of discipline.

January 1989

On taking action:

On the one hand, whatever you are doing at a given moment, you must treat it as the most important thing to be done at that moment in time. This requires you to be convinced that it is indeed the most important task that needs to be done. The second part of the proposition is the problem: if you are not convinced, the question will bother you and will not let you concentrate on the task, and your performance will suffer. Hence, once you decide which task to perform, you must not second guess yourself (this is a unique feature of this particular type of decision process).

- During training, always try to challenge your soldiers by placing them in situations they have never encountered before. But during military operations or in battle, caution must be taken, since the difference between a challenging situation and an impossible one is very small.
- When taking action, it is better to make a mistake than to be paralyzed with indecision. Combat experience reduces the soldiers' anxiety. At the same time it sharpens their fear – which is an advantage. Anxiety paralyzes the soldiers, while fear propels them to (some kind of) action.

March 1989

On morale:

I do not believe morale is the most important parameter. True, it is an important part of a unit's ability to perform a mission (any mission) successfully. Nevertheless, it does not have to be equally high at all times. Sometimes morale has to be lowered, even artificially, in order to achieve better results.

- Positive reinforcement is effective when I want to motivate someone to **do** something; negative reinforcement is effective when I want to motivate them to **avoid** a certain action.
- Responsibility cannot be shared; blame, on the other hand, can be.

April 1989

When fighting on the Lebanon border, it is crucial to win each and every battle. In the Intifada, on the other hand, it is sometimes warranted to lose a battle, even deliberately, in order to win the war.

June 1989

On the sanctity of orders:

Four dimensions sanctify justify a commander's order: the fact it was given, the fact it was received, its content and its spirit.

Common errors while giving commands:

Vagueness (out of a desire to leave the decision to your subordinates), and citing superior officers ("the general said...")

In theory, you must always be faithful both to both the **letter** and the **spirit** of an order. But in practice, an order must be followed to the letter when, and only when, it precisely suits the situation in which you are operating and the goal you are to achieve. When the situation and the goal are new, you must be faithful to the spirit of the order by doing whatever you consider will lead to the attainment of the goal.

But what if the precise wording of an order is at odds with its spirit? (And this does happen!) In this situation, the commander must employ his own judgment. Hence, though orders are indeed sacred, their sanctity justification is not absolute, and cannot be the foundation of the entire structure of the army.

July-August 1989

On loyalty:

On the full meaning of loyalty – to subordinates and to superior officers:
Loyalty to superior officers means that, when you hand down their orders to your subordinates, you present every order as though you yourself decided on it. Never say "the commander said."

Loyalty to your subordinates means that, when discussing their failures or errors with your superiors, you take responsibility upon yourself and describe the mistakes as your own. You must shift the focus to yourself – even if later, when facing the erring subordinate, you will hold him fully responsible for his actions.

Following your superior officers' orders – in word and in spirit – is an integral part of your loyalty to them. A commander who does not follow orders will not be obeyed by his own subordinates (because he has given them the impression that orders are not to be followed).

September 1989

A lesson in decision-making:

Decisions

Today I received a most important lesson from Brigade Commander Ravve on making decisions, namely that a decision must always be made by the commander who has the greatest amount of information on the variables affecting the decision. In other words, the person making the decision must meet two conditions. First, he must be a commander, so that he will have a broad perspective on of the situation. Second, he must possess the greatest amount of relevant information. Hence, a brigade commander may give an order directly to a company commander, without involving the battalion commander. Another corollary, of course, is that in battle a platoon commander or company commander may make a decision, and in real time you will have no choice but to approve it (since you know less about the situation than he does).

October 1989

The IDF's operations in the West Bank are meant to address the outward expressions of a phenomenon and not against the phenomenon itself (the phenomenon being the Palestinian's desire for an independent state). The phenomenon itself will never go away. What might disappear – for a limited time period – are its outward expressions.

November 1989

- In some situations, the most powerful statement is silence. Similarly, in some situations the best action is inaction.

- A commander's problem in the West Bank is that he must provide solutions that are acceptable to both the radical right and the radical left. The Torah was right in saying, "You shall not plow with an ox and a donkey yoked together." Rashi stresses that this rule applies not only to plowing but to hauling any kind of load.

On motivation:

The one motivating force that must always be at the highest possible level is cohesion. Cohesion = discipline + morale + sense of belonging. But that is not all. The saying that the whole is always greater than the sum of its parts is true here as well.

Managing consciousness:

Managing consciousness is an important and complicated part of the art of command. In times of calm, it is possible to conduct surveys among the troops to find out their opinion on various matters; in times of war, a commander's sensitivity to the thoughts and feelings of his soldiers is of utmost importance. Such sensitivity often requires a commander to take an action that is tactically wrong but necessary from the point of view of consciousness, in order to best promote the achievement of the goal. For instance, in battle a commander may need to risk himself just in order to show his troops that he is willing to do so.

December 1989

More on motivation:

There are two modes of command on the battlefield: the "sweeping" mode and the "pushing" mode. The former has more advantages, but there are situations where a commander must employ the latter. An example of the "sweeping" mode of command is when a company commander needs only to climb into a tank and take off for the whole company to follow him (Hanan).

A battle that requires the employment of the pushing mode is the most complicated kind of battle (in terms of the commander's motivating abilities). Assault breaching is an example: you cannot take the place of the vehicles with mine-rollers and mine-clearing line charges – you have no choice but to send them ahead. In such a battle, you must demonstrate your willingness to take personal risks – even if this is not tactically necessary and if your getting wounded will only hurt the mission (good examples of commanders who did this are Moshe Dayan and Douglas MacArthur).

January 1990

Some company commanders do the right thing (Hanan) and some do things the right way (Eyal and Ofer), but some do the right thing the right way (Avishai).

February 1990

The commander must not be a technocrat or a bureaucrat

The commander must develop a complete emotional bond with his unit. His emotions are an integral part of his ability to function; it is they that provide him with certain qualities and abilities that his intelligence alone cannot provide. When a commander loves his unit he feels is sensitive to it and knows what he can obtain from it, but also knows when he cannot push any harder. Due to this and other considerations, emotional ability is an important part of a commander's overall performance.

When I tried to envision my performance as a battalion commander, I pictured a tiger on the hunt, following his inner voice (intuition!?). I made decisions by looking inward in a natural, almost bestial way, not through any kind of mathematical rational calculating.

- Planning is the most important part of doing. Its importance derives precisely from what we call flexibility of performance.

On change:

Some consider change as being an end in itself. They must show me a change that does not evoke the question "what for?" (The purpose of an action is the answer to the question "what for?"). As long as this question cannot be answered, change cannot be considered an end in itself.

A change in plan costs energy (to the unit that performs it), because it requires the battalion commander to explain the new plan to the company commander, the staff, the brigade, the neighboring forces, etc.). Hence, a change must be introduced only if it clearly yields an advantage whose value on the battlefield justifies the energy expended by the battalion.

Clearly, a commander must be open to change and must devise plans which are strong enough to withstand change. The danger does not lie in making an occasional change, but in ending up with constant changes in what had once been a plan. (Where is the line between flexibility of thought and baseless thinking?)

March 1990

- One of the problems in finding a measure for assessing effectiveness is neutralizing the impact of external circumstances on the battalion.

- Often it is important to lower demands in performing one mission (and thus perform it less well) in order to increase the unit's preparedness for the next mission.

- He who decentralizes authority loses authority; he who delegates authority can always take it back.

- A crucial condition for making progress (in terms of quality) is the assumption that "any action can be performed better". This assumption creates the correct climate for dissecting past actions, learning from mistakes and applying the lesson to future actions.

June 1990

- Inflexibility as a personality trait provides a wide range of abilities for manipulating others, but it tends to seep into one's thoughts and evolve into mental rigidity, which is a limitation. People must be taught to be unbendable in character but flexible in their thinking (implementing this combination in practice is a real art).

Lack of rigidity in a commander transforms him into a "mailman." This is the worst type of commander: one who is constantly busy relaying his soldiers' messages to his superior officers and the messages of his superiors to his soldiers. Commanders like these have no right to exist and must not remain in their position for even a moment.

Professionalism

- A common error, which is endemic to the IDF historically, is to think that the battalion commander or company commander must be the best gunner in the company or the battalion. In practice, the battalion commander must be the best battalion commander in the battalion, and the company commander must be the best company commander in the company.

An officer at the level of battalion commander or higher (and perhaps even at the level of company commander) does not have to know every nut and bolt in a tank. It's more important for him to know what a tank can and cannot perform.

To be a good trainer of gunners, one does not need to be a very good gunner. One must be very good at training gunners.

The job of the commander on the battlefield is to be a commander, not a gunner, and therefore he must focus in his training on becoming a commander, not a gunner.

July-August 1990

What does it mean to have your soldiers trust you?

It means that they assume – unconsciously – that everything

you do you do for a reason, and that, if there is a problem, you must have done everything in your power to eliminate it.

- Rigidity is a good quality, but pigheadedness is also a kind of rigidity.

September 1990

The commander's self-consciousness:

In a meeting about the list of assignments, Oren (the staff officer for personnel support, the S1) made a suggestion and I immediately shot it down. Later that night it bugged me. I asked myself whether I had rejected his suggestion because it was bad, or just because it came from him.

Every commander or manager knows the feeling that comes with making an non-objective decision, and every commander and manager would be happy to avoid making such decisions.

One thing that happens when you work with your staff and your subordinate officers, is that when one of the people you respect less or like less makes a suggestion, something inside you does not let you judge the suggestion objectively. Your opinion of the man strongly biases your opinion of his suggestion. The opposite is also true, of course. If you like and respect a person, it is easier to accept his opinions. This actually makes sense. You appreciate a person because you trust his opinions and reasoning. Still, it is wise to consider every suggestion on its own merit. It is at times like these that I wish I had a psychologist beside me (or anyone else who knew knows to ask the right questions). He would help me to be more introspective and to determine if my judgement of the suggestion stems from my opinion of the man. By asking the right questions, I think it is possible to reach a point where the commander (or manager) considers every proposal on its merit, regardless of who suggested it. By reaching this point we considerably improve our decisions: we avoid both errors of omission (needlessly rejecting suggestions by subordinates we appreciate less) and errors of commission (accepting bad suggestions by those we esteem).

- My initial assumption was that some companies are better suited for certain tasks while other units are better suited for other tasks, and that the same is true for commanders: one commander is better at task A and another at task B. However, to my surprise, this assumption was not borne out by reality. No tasks can be more dissimilar than activity on the Lebanon border and operational activity in the West Bank. Yet, despite this, commanders tended to display a nearly identical level of competence at both tasks. For this reason, I began attributing less importance to the nature of the task, and concentrated mainly on matching the commander to the company, knowing that, if the match was good, they would be able to handle any task assigned to them.

In order to completely neutralize the impact of external circumstances – i.e., the nature of the task – the *structure* of the task must be suited to the company commander. One commander may be better at taking target X from the right, while another commander will be better at taking this that target from the front. But one commander will not be better suited than the other to the task itself (assuming that the commanders are similar in their overall level of competence, albeit different in their traits).

My conclusion is that emphasis must be placed on the commander and the company. Examine the commander, examine the company, and assess to what extent they match each other. If they are well-matched, they will successfully achieve any goal.

October 1990

Passed the baton of commandership to Mati.

Conclusions upon completing my role

- No goal justifies all ends, and no value can be regarded as absolute.

- **Fundamental assumption**: Everything that was done could have been done better.

- Never place your subordinates in situations that are impossible for them to handle.

BIBLIOGRAPHY

Amir, Udi, *Battle Command and Procedure at the Battalion Level* (Ground Corps Command – Doctrine and Development Department, Warfighting Doctrine Branch, 1989).

Aristotle, *Nicomachean Ethics*, trans. Joseph Gerhard Liebes (Tel Aviv: Schocken, 1985).

Aristotle, *Metaphysics*, trans. W. D. Ross (Internet Classics Archive, http://classics.mit.edu/Aristotle/metaphysics.html, accessed May 2015).

Ben-Israel, Isaac, *Dialogues on Science and Military Intelligence* (Tel Aviv: IDF Publishing House, Maarachot, 1989).

Caspi, Moshe D., *Who Thinks?* (Ramat Gan: Massada, 1978).

Ginsburg, Shimona (ed.), *Sources in the Philosophy of Science* (Tel Aviv: Open University, Center for Educational Technology, 1977).
Janis, Irving L. and Leon Mann, *Decision Making: A Psychological Analysis of Conflict, Choice and Commitment* (New York: Free Press, 1977).

Kotler, Philip, *Principles of Marketing,* Englewood Cliffs, NJ: Prentice-Hall, 1980).

Menuchin, Ishai (ed.), On *Democracy* and *Obedience* (Jerusalem: the Yesh Gvul Movement and Siman Kriah Books, 1990).

PUM Barak Program, *Situation Estimate* (IDF Operations Department/Instruction Division/Warfighting Doctrine Branch, 1990).

Schwartz, Hanan, *Holistic and Procedural Thinking: New Wine in an Old Bottle* (unpublished manuscript).

Wittgenstein, Ludwig, *Tractatus Logico-Philosophicus*, trans. Eddy Zemach (Tel Aviv: Hakibbutz HaMeuchad, 1994).

Yair, Yoram (Yaya), *With Me from Lebanon* (Tel Aviv: IDF Publishing House, Maarachot, 1990).

Zakai, Dan, "Decisions, Decisions, Decisions..." In: *Skira Hodshit* (Monthly Survey), May 1984, pp. 3-11.

www.ingramcontent.com/pod-product-compliance
Lightning Source LLC
Chambersburg PA
CBHW070014110426
42741CB00034B/1793